Folklore Rules

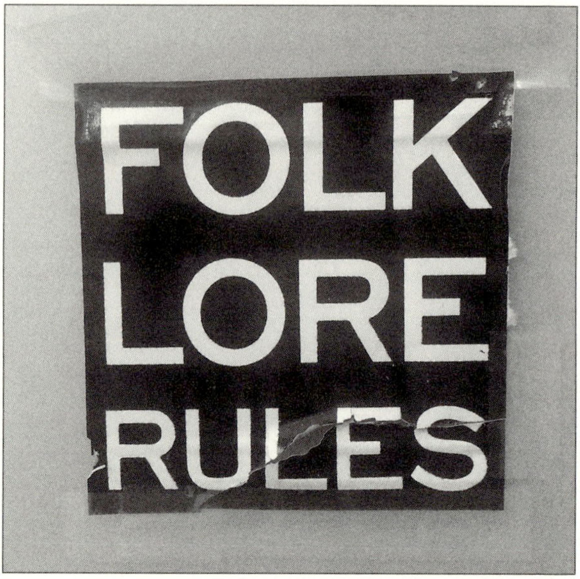
FOLK
LORE
RULES

Folklore Rules

A Fun, Quick, and Useful Introduction to
the Field of Academic Folklore Studies

Lynne S. McNeill

Utah State University Press
Logan

© 2013 by University Press of Colorado

Published by Utah State University Press
An imprint of University Press of Colorado
5589 Arapahoe Avenue, Suite 206C
Boulder, Colorado 80303

All rights reserved
Printed in the United States of America

 The University Press of Colorado is a proud member of
the Association of American University Presses.

The University Press of Colorado is a cooperative publishing enterprise supported,
in part, by Adams State University, Colorado State University, Fort Lewis College,
Metropolitan State University of Denver, Regis University, University of Colorado,
University of Northern Colorado, Utah State University, and Western State Colorado
University.

∞ This paper meets the requirements of the ANSI/NISO Z39.48-1992 (Permanence
of Paper).

Figure 4.1, "Omikuji," is courtesy of Alex Anderson (abanderson.com). Figures
4.2–4.7 are based on Allie Brosh's *Hyperbole and a Half.*

Library of Congress Cataloging-in-Publication Data
McNeill, Lynne S.
  Folklore rules / Lynne S. McNeill.
    pages cm
  ISBN 978-0-87421-905-0 (hardback) — ISBN 978-0-87421-906-7 (e-book)
  1. Folklore—Study and teaching. I. Title.
  GR45.M36 2013
  398.2071—dc23
                                    2013019566

Cover illustrations, clockwise from top: Alex Anderson (abanderson.com), "Omikuji"; Van E. Porter, "Zonnie 'Grandma' Johnson and Barre Toelken"; © Allie Brosh
(hyperboleandahalf.blogspot.com); Zander Westendarp, "Guanajuato 2013."

For Barre Toelken

Contents

Preface

THE FIELD OF FOLKLORE STUDIES HAS HAD A fascinating and complicated history, growing out of and blending several different established areas of study. It is also, for all its seeming simplicity, a very complicated field to sum up and explain; the fact that definitions for *folklore* are still being created and debated well over 100 years after the term was coined proves this. On a related note, the field has also long been suffering from a prolonged and depressing identity crisis, one that each new generation of scholars has inherited and must come to terms with, and one that is, unfortunately, often foisted upon students.

The reality is that folklore, as a field of study, is cool. Students know this, they can sense it, and when they find themselves in a class reading a textbook that right from the get-go tries to account for all the difficulty in definition, all the ambiguity of placement in the academy, all the questions of naming and whatnot, they're disappointed. The field needs a textbook that lets folklore be both fun *and* complicated. *Folklore Rules* doesn't deny the academic rigor of the field; it simply shows new students that there is something both coherent and, yes, cool, to be studied here. Once students buy into that, chewing over the complexities actually becomes fun.

The field also needs a textbook that's relatively short; it's not always feasible to take an entire semester introducing new students to the field of folklore studies. Many folklorists are not employed in departments that offer generalized folklore courses; when they teach folklore-related classes, they are often special-topics courses that throw unsuspecting and unprepared students into a field that is new to them but to which there is no time to offer a full introduction. Even at schools with a folklore program there are not always prerequisites for upper-division folklore courses, so there's no way to ensure that students are familiar with the field in general before launching into a focused special-topics course.

A concise text that introduces students to the field of folklore studies without overwhelming them with case studies or with the complexity of the field's history will allow students to become familiar with the field quickly but accurately, thus gaining a better understanding of how the topic they're studying in class is contextualized in the larger field of study. It is a common complaint among graduate students, many of whom do not have undergraduate backgrounds in folklore, that while they become experts on their thesis topics, they don't have a basic understanding of the breadth of the field. This textbook hopes to ameliorate that situation as well, providing an enjoyable and concise introduction to the basics of folklore studies.

Acknowledgments

For a superb grounding in the discipline of folklore, I owe my thanks to Alan Dundes, Dan Melia, John Lindow, Jeannie Thomas, Barre Toelken, Steve Siporin, Randy Williams, Elliott Oring, Michael Owen Jones, Polly Stewert, Cathy Preston, Paul Smith, Peter Narváez, Jerry Pocius, Martin Lovelace, and Diane Goldstein. For their support, guidance, friendship, consideration, scholarship, and time, I would also like to thank Ian Brodie, Jodi McDavid, Andrea Kitta, Tok Thompson, Nelda Ault, Trevor Blank, John Alley, and Michael Spooner. Thanks are due to Matt Bradley for inspiring the title; his enthusiasm for folklore lives on. Special thanks also go to my parents, Mike and Lysbeth McNeill, and to my husband, Stephen VanGeem. I'm lucky to know and to have known so many incredible people.

For the Instructor
Why You Want to Use This Book

A MAJOR ISSUE IN THE TEACHING OF FOLKLORE THESE days is that folklore programs are few and far between. Many folklorists are working not in dedicated folklore programs but in English, anthropology, history, or communications departments, and while that highlights the incredible interdisciplinarity of our field, it presents an interesting quandary to many instructors.

Without a dedicated folklore program, students are likely to encounter folklore courses randomly, taking an upper-division, special-topic, "Folklore and Fill-in-the-Blank" (film, literature, history, etc.) course without ever having taken Introduction to Folklore. This is great on the one hand, as it helps students discover the field. On the other hand, it means that students are showing up in highly specialized folklore courses without any concept of the basics of folklore studies (or worse, with an incorrect or misguided concept of folklore studies).

There are several great intro textbooks out there for folklore students, but they all share one thing in common: they're long. As any folklorist can tell you, folklore sounds simple, but isn't. Most introductory textbooks are way too long for students to consume and comprehend in the mere week or two that their professors can sacrifice to getting everyone on the same page about the basics before moving on to the specific topic of the course.

Other fields don't have this problem in the same way, because other fields aren't quite so unfamiliar to the general public as academic disciplines. Even without taking Introduction to Literature, most college students can join in a "Literature and Fill-in-the-Blank" (the West, race, identity, etc.) course without being too far out of the loop. Even if they're not totally prepared, they at least learned the generic distinctions between a poem and a play in high school. Try asking a college student who hasn't taken an Introduction to Folklore class the difference between a folktale and a legend, and you're not likely to get a correct answer. It's simply not a subject that's mainstream enough (though we all know it should be) to go forward without an introduction to the basics.

Enter this book. It's short, it's simple, and, most important, it's true to the field of academic folklore studies. Students will get a sense of the basics—the accurate basics, not the foreshortened it's-not-just-old-wives'-tales-and-quilting-but-that's-all-we-have-time-for basics—without having to read an entire lengthy textbook.

For the sake of brevity, you're not going to find a whole lot of drawn-out or exotic case studies here—that's not the point of this book. What this book does offer is relatable, illustrative scenarios, ones that will make students feel closer to the field rather than farther away from it. And that's not to say that there's no room for any extended examples to grow out of this book; bringing students' own experiences in as concrete case studies should be quite easy.

In fact, this is one of the greatest things about folklore studies: students show up knowing some folklore, even if they don't yet know they know it. This is due to the unique fact that folklorists (and folklore students) are, across the board, also members of the folk. As folklorist Jay Mechling once noted, thinking like a folklorist involves "a sort of 'double consciousness' about everyday life"[1]— participating in it normally and yet simultaneously stepping back to observe it critically. Very few other fields of study allow for this dual level of engagement, especially in the humanities.[2] How many Shakespeare classes can say that 100 percent of incoming students show up already knowing (not to mention ready to perform) at least two or three Shakespeare plays inside and out? None.[3] Folklore has the advantage,[4] as all students have at least some folklore in their lives and so can immediately begin applying cool analyses and theories to stuff they already know about. I find that this leads to a higher engagement in folklore classes than in almost any other course that deals with the analysis of culture or literature—the analysis is the fun and challenging stuff, and folklore students are able to jump right in.

In addition to the preponderance of highly specific special-topics classes and a glaring lack of required introductory courses, the field of folklore studies also suffers from another unique problem. In general, folklorists are really into validating/justifying/illustrating-the-nuanced-complexities-of the field in the face of perceived judgment from more universally recognized academic programs. This is great, but let's consider the student's perspective—it's one heck of a complicated field. While it certainly can all come together in the end (fairly simply, too), a rundown of all the famous and infamous attempts to account for all the ambiguities and complexities up front often leads to turning a really, really awesome subject into the driest of all dry classes.[5] Students find themselves looking around, going, "Hey, I thought this was a folklore class! Isn't it supposed to be fun and easy?" While we shouldn't say yes to the latter, we should absolutely be saying yes to the former: folklore is fun. Period. And students need to know that.

I can relate to the need to successfully sum up the entirety of folklore studies. When I was a student I kept a notebook (three, actually, by the time I was done with school), and every time I came across a great summary of the field, I'd write it in there and try to memorize it, mainly so I could explain to my relatives at the holidays what, exactly, I was studying. Most students, myself included, don't achieve such succinctness until the end of their studies, and it's easy for all the fun stuff to get momentarily lost in the lack of simplicity.

So here's the thing: folklore is fun and yes, its complexities and depths and nuances and difficulties need to be addressed and comprehended, but let's be honest: it should be fun first, to let students know why exactly they'll want to spend the rest of their lives (or at least the rest of the semester) thinking about all the complexities. As an instructor, although I want my initial explanation of folklore to my students to be academically impressive, I want it to be interesting and engaging, too.

Folklorists also have a tendency to overstate the complexities of the field, especially to new audiences. The downside of the name "folklore" is that it's an easily trivialized concept (by people who don't fully understand it, at least), and it appears that most folklorists shy away from any explanation of the field that could potentially support this trivialization. Thus, we get incoherent, excessively qualified, overwrought explanations of a field that, whether we like it or not, *does* have some basic rules.

This book is designed to present those rules in a user-friendly manner and to serve in a variety of capacities: as a quick reference guide for an intro class, as the introductory reading for a special-topics class, as a reminder of the basics for grad students, as a gift for relatives who still don't get what it is you do. Its whole purpose is to help nonfolklorists "get it" initially, so that they're ready to move on to deeper or related issues.

Set to teach a class on traditional English Morris dancing? Great! Contextualize it within the field of folklore studies with this handy book! Want to assign a grad class the forty-two great articles that shaped the field of folklore as we know it? Great! Use this handy book as a simple background guide. There will be plenty of time for you to nuance and problematize all the information here, so take the opportunity initially to make it seem more straightforward.

Personally, I found that the famous foundational works made the most sense to me after I was done with my PhD anyway, when I was finally ready to admire the simplicity those scholars strove to achieve with their theories and definitions. So use this book as you will, and never let yourself lose sight of (or fail to pass on to students) the very first reason you chose to study folklore: folklore rules.

NOTES

1. Jay Mechling, "How Do You Know What You Know?" *Working Papers of the Ohio State University Center for Folklore Studies* 2, no. 3 (October 2011), https://kb.osu.edu/dspace/handle/1811/46895.

2. Psychology, a field that folklore studies often utilizes when divining the motivation behind tradition, is perhaps the most similar in this regard.

3. Okay, I'll admit I didn't research that one. But it makes for a dramatic sentence, doesn't it? And it's probably true.

4. Yes, this book is shamelessly pro-folklore.

5. I know this, because I've done it myself.

Folklore Rules

Chapter 1

What Is Folklore?

So, you're in a folklore class. Good for you—whatever educational requirement this course is fulfilling for you, I guarantee you've picked the best possible way to fulfill it. Perhaps you're in an Intro to Folklore course, or maybe you're in a special-topics course: something like Folklore and Literature, Folklore and Film, Folklore and the Internet, or Children's Folklore. No matter what course it is (and hey—maybe you're not taking a folklore class at all. Maybe you're not even a student, in which case, doubly good for you for reading this book when you don't have to!), you're going to have to start at the beginning. Unlike in other fields, when it comes to folklore studies, the beginning can sometimes be the most confusing place to start.

What is folklore? You'd think this would be an easy question to answer. "Folklore" doesn't seem like a very complicated idea, does it? I mean, it's not a rare or unfamiliar word—we use it fairly often in daily life. So if someone asked you what folklore is, you could probably give them an answer, right? Well . . . maybe not. Give it a try and see how it goes. Lots of people answer this question by giving a few examples of stuff they think is folklore. They'll say something like, "Oh, you know, folklore is old stories and songs from your parents and grandparents" or "Folklore is stuff like superstitions and old wives' tales" or "It's like unicorns and sea shanties and quilting—stuff like that."

As you will learn shortly, while these common perceptions of folklore aren't 100 percent wrong, they're certainly not 100

DOI: 10.7330/9780874219067.c001

percent right, either. One of the first things that students of folk-lore discover is that the word *folklore* encompasses far more than they ever thought it did. It brings together the expected folktales, myths, and legends, and yet also includes jump-rope rhymes, pranks, jokes, graffiti, songs, emoticons, gestures . . . basically a ton of stuff that often leads to the popular first-year-folklore-student mistake of "I get it now—folklore is everything!" This, sadly, is not true. You'll see by the end of this book that while folklore can likely be connected to almost everything, everything is not, in fact, folklore.

Folklorists have spent a fairly ridiculous amount of time try-ing to succinctly define folklore ever since the word was coined in 1846[1] by a guy named William Thoms. Thoms, interestingly, used a pseudonym (he chose Ambrose Merton, for some reason) when he proposed the term and revealed himself as the actual source of the term only once he'd determined that people were generally on board with it. He proposed it as "a good Saxon compound" in favor of the then current term *popular antiquities.* People generally accepted it, and voila!—a whole field of study was born.[2]

You might be wondering at this point why it has been so hard for folklorists to define this basic Saxon compound. Well, you try to explain what a creation myth, a jump-rope rhyme, a Fourth of July BBQ, and some bathroom graffiti[3] have in common, and you'll find it's not a terribly easy task, either. Rest assured, though: the field of folklore studies does have a few basic rules that can help to simplify things. In the next few sections, we're going to uncover these basic concepts from within the murky depths of academia and put them to work to answer the question at hand: "What is folklore?"

FOLK AND LORE

To start with, we've got a compound word here—folk-lore—and any decent definition will have to account for both parts.[4] We'll start with "folk." In order to begin to understand what "folk" means, we first need to back up a bit and understand what "culture" is. Why, you ask? Because I said so. Bear with me—it will become clear in a moment.

As it turns out, in terms of difficulty of definition, "culture" is frustratingly right up there with "folklore." A common use of the word *culture* is to think of someone as being "cultured," as in "enlightened" or "refined"—snooty people attending the opera in fur coats and such—but folklorists (and anthropologists) use the term a bit differently. There have been whole books written on the definition of culture, but since this guide is meant to be short and straightforward, I'm just going to give you one of the most useful ones, created by an anthropologist named Ward Goodenough (and yes, you can insert a pun about it being a "good enough" definition here). He tells us: "A society's culture is whatever it is one has to know or believe in order to act in a manner acceptable to its members."[5]

This definition tells us several things right off the bat. First, that culture is something that a society, or a group of people, possesses. Second, that culture isn't really a tangible object, but more of a body of knowledge. "Acting in a manner that's acceptable" to a group of people encompasses a ton of information: you have to know official things, like on which side of the road to drive, what currency you use to pay for stuff, where you can and cannot be naked—all the things that would get you arrested if you did them wrong. But there's a more subtle or informal level to "acceptable" behavior, too—stuff that may not get you arrested if you do it wrong, but that may earn you some weird looks and cause people to cross the street to get away from you.

For example, if you just openly picked your nose while your boss was talking to you, or if you greeted your date's parents by passionately kissing them, or if you sat down at a table in McDonald's and tried to flag down a server to come and take your order—these are all things that our informal culture tells us are incorrect ways to act. There's no official big book about how or how not to do these things; we learn the right way to do them simply by observation, by spending time in our society, and often these expectations are so ingrained in us that we don't notice them until we go somewhere where people do them differently.

There's no official regulation or documentation of how (and how not) to greet strangers—we learn it by observation and experience.

Fast-food restaurants don't print manuals about how and where to order—we learn it informally, by watching our friends or parents go through the line ahead of us when we're kids. It's interesting to note that when we travel to other cultures, it's rarely the official differences (the language, the currency, the laws) that make us feel out of place—we expect those things to be different when we travel. It's the little stuff—the informal stuff, like how to greet people, or whether to order at the counter or wait to be seated, or how close to stand to strangers on a bus—that really makes us feel far from home.

This informal or unofficial level of cultural understanding is the "folk" level, the level on which cultural knowledge is shared, enacted, and propagated by regular, everyday people. Instead of laws we have customs; instead of guidebooks we have experience and observation.

In the past, when scholars talked about the "folk," they were referring to a distinct class of people: typically rural, uneducated, illiterate peasants. Today when we use the term we're simply talking about everyone, all of us, as we exist in the informal or unofficial realms of our cultural lives.

Thus, when folklorists talk about a "folk group," they're not talking about a certain type of people; they're talking about all people who share an unofficial culture together. In fact, the most popular definition of a folk group these days is "any group of people whatsoever who share at least one common factor."[6] That's pretty broad, isn't it? By this definition, a family is a folk group, as is a campus community or a neighborhood. An entire religion can form a folk group, as can the population of an individual synagogue, temple, or parish. A folk group can be national, ethnic, regional, occupational, interest-based—basically anything that unites people and generates a shared cultural understanding. Folk groups can be small, with just a few members,[7] or huge, with hundreds of thousands of people included.

Many of these groups clearly have an institutional culture as well as a folk culture—campuses, churches, occupations, states, and nations will have both official and unofficial aspects of their culture—and when we refer to those groups as a "folk group," we're purposefully focusing on their unofficial realm. In contrast, some groups don't have much of an institutional culture at all—friend groups and families are typically entirely folk or informal[8] in their cultural existence and expression. It's a useful distinction to make, especially when seeking to avoid the "Folklore is everything!" fallacy.

Right away it should be easy to see that all of us are members of many folk groups all at once, and it takes only a moment of reflection to understand that we use different sets of folk cultural knowledge when we're with those different groups. There's often slang or terminology that you use at school or at work that you don't use at home, not necessarily because it's vulgar or inappropriate, but just because no one at home would know what it means—they're not in that other group; they wouldn't "get it." There are songs you sing at church that you don't sing at work, because those songs aren't a part of your job's folk culture. There are people who use thicker accents at home than at work, and people who dress one way at certain types of events (like football games) and another way at other types of events (like dinner parties). You won't get arrested for wearing a cocktail dress to a football game (or face paint to a dinner party), but it's not the cultural norm. Our awareness of our many overlapping folk groups allows us to adapt ourselves appropriately to different cultural situations.

So that's the "folk" part of "folklore"—the unofficial and informal levels of a group's culture, in which we all participate in a number of intersecting and overlapping circles. But what about the "lore"?

Well, "lore" is what gives form to folklore. Rather than simply being the general shared awareness of how to behave in a group or a society, folklore comprises the specific expressive forms that a group uses to communicate and interact. We call these forms the genres of folklore, and just as literature students study different genres of literature (poems, plays, novellas) or film students study different genres of film (drama, comedy, action-adventure), folklorists study different genres of folklore, such as customs, narratives, and beliefs (there are a lot more than just these three—we'll discuss this more in depth in chapter 3). While many folklorists are certainly interested in the generalized folk culture of a group, they commonly focus their work on one or more of the expressive genres that a folk group produces and shares.

As later chapters in this handbook will show you, the genres of folklore are typically divided into different types of expressive forms (some genres are in the form of narratives, some are customary behaviors, some are conceptual, etc.). For now, given our current goal of defining folklore in general, we can set that aside and think about what separates all kinds of folklore from all other types of cultural expression. Because, of course, while we have folk customs and folk music and folk stories, we also have legal procedures, symphonies, novels, plays, TV shows and the like, and we need to consider what sets "folklore" apart from these other forms of cultural expression.

Well, if you were paying attention just a few paragraphs ago, you'll likely remember that "folk" culture is the informal or unofficial parts of culture. It makes sense, then, to say that "folk anything" (folk stories, folk music, folk customs) are the unofficial instances of those things. "Folk" becomes an adjective that applies to "lore": What kind of lore? Folk-lore!

For example, if we're talking about a story it's easy to see that "stories" can occur in both folk and official ways: our culture has not only folktales and urban legends, but also comic books and mystery novels. The former are folklore; the latter are not. Similarly, we have not only folk songs, but pop songs and symphonies, too. Not only do we have folk customs, but we have laws and governmental regulations.

The thing that distinguishes folklore from these other forms of cultural expression *is the way it's transmitted.* (You can tell by the fact that those words are italicized that they're important—you should probably write that part down in your notes.) For all that we might try to define folklore by what it is, it's actually much more clearly defined by how it's used and shared. We can't simply say that folklore is stories, because so are TV shows and so are novels. The difference is in how the story moves through a population.[9]

VARIATION AND TRADITION

In folk culture, the lore is typically shared by word of mouth; more generally, we can say it's shared person to person (which could include direct conversation, indirect observation, e-mail, phone calls, online chats, etc.). So, I tell an urban legend to a few of my friends, and they in turn tell it to some people they know, who in turn tell it to others, who then pass it on to more people, and so on. A good analogy is the game "telephone"—a bunch of kids sit in a circle and someone starts off a message by whispering it to the person next to him or her, who then whispers it to the next person, and so on. The main difference between folklore and the telephone game is that folklore doesn't go in a tidy circle. If we were to draw the folk process of transmission, it might look like this:

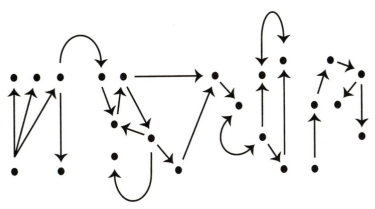

Fig. 1.1

Lots of people are hearing the same story, but most of them hear it from a different source. In contrast, the mass- or pop-culture model has lots and lots of people hearing the same story from a single source, such as the television, a news website, or a published book. Millions of people might all watch the same show, but they all get it from the same source, and so the version they all get is identical. This process might look like this:

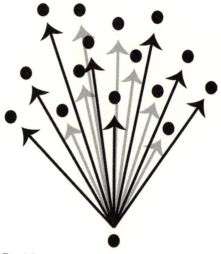

Fig. 1.2

The differences between these two modes of transmission are pretty obvious. Even if the same number of people end up hearing the folk story as watch the TV show or read the book, the folk story was told and retold anew all along the way. And it probably changed a bit as it was told over and over again, just like the message in the telephone game, the point of which, as you probably recall, was always to compare the final message to the original, to see the (hopefully hilarious) ways it evolved during transmission. The study of folklore is pretty much the same thing (minus the expectation of hilarity).

With a TV show or a published book, every single person who watches or reads the story gets the exact same version, and that single version is usually tied to a specific director or writer. With a folk story, each new audience gets a unique, contextually specific version, and each new teller is as much the rightful "owner" as the next. This, of course, is what makes folklore so interesting. If I tell you a joke, and you turn around and tell it to someone else and the details change a bit, you didn't tell it wrong, you just told a different version of it.[10] You also didn't steal it from me—you might tell your friends where you heard it, but even if you don't, I don't get to file a copyright lawsuit against you. Folklore is mostly anonymous,[11] so it can easily belong to whoever is telling it. In contrast, if I take a novel and change some of the words, it's not just "another version" or "my own version" of the novel; it's wrong. If I went out and sold "my version" of the novel, I could be arrested.

So folklore, by the nature of its transmission, is malleable, adaptable, changeable, and mostly anonymous, and this makes it way more culturally and expressively communicative than a TV show. I don't get to alter an episode of TV to make it more relevant to my life, but I can alter an urban legend or a joke in order to make it more specific to me and my situation. Considering that folklore is being slightly adapted and molded every time it's passed on, after a while it's quite representative of the group as a whole rather than of a single individual. The stuff that no one found meaningful or illustrative or entertaining will eventually get leeched out, and the stuff that most people thought was especially important or relevant or significant will remain in. Group consensus shapes folklore, and so folklore is a great measure of group consensus.

There's another level of culture in which any given expressive genre can emerge, and that's "elite" culture. It's more like pop culture than folk culture, but the audience is typically smaller as the content is typically thought to have less of a broad appeal. This is where we find the expressive forms that we tend to think of as "snooty" and limited to highly educated audiences: the opera, modern art museums, symphonies, and so on. If we drew a model of this one, it might look like this:

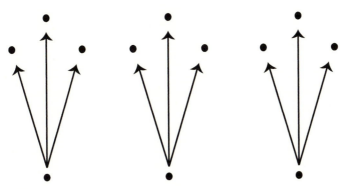

Fig. 1.3

There's not just a single source, as there is with pop culture—different ballet companies can all perform the same famous ballet and each company's production will be slightly different—but there's not the numerous and accessible re-creations of the folk method of transmission either. You can see how a single expressive form, like a drawing, a story, or a song, could emerge in each of the three different levels: as graffiti, a comic book, and a museum piece; as a folktale, a romance novel, and a literary novel; and as a children's rhyme, a pop song, and a symphony, respectively. The difference isn't so much in the form; it's in the way that form is transmitted within a population.

Now, we need to make something clear here: there's no judgment intended in comparing "folk" culture to "popular" and "elite" culture—once upon a time elite culture may have been considered "better" than folk culture, but that's a thing of the past. These are terms that describe transmission, not ascribe value. And in fact, these categories really aren't all that clear-cut. Is this tidy three-level breakdown an oversimplification? Totally. Are these categories permeable and inconsistent? Yup. Can stuff move from one level to another, or exist in two at the same time? Of course! This model is a useful tool for illustrating how folk forms of expression move through a population differently than other forms, but in truth, these categories are quite permeable and vague.

Consider, for example, the number of symphonic melodies that are used and shared in a folk way. Many of us hum the first few notes of Beethoven's 5th Symphony when we want to indicate that something dramatic has happened or is about to happen—*dun-dun-dun-DUN*—and most of us do that because we've heard others do it, not because we attended the symphony. Pop culture gets in on the action, too: remember that lilting melody that always accompanied Porky Pig when he skipped through a lovely nature scene? That's Humoresque No. 7 in G flat major, by Dvorak. The folk can also borrow from pop culture: how many of us have whistled the theme to *Gilligan's Island* when we thought a trip was going poorly? So we can clearly have a folk appropriation of elite and pop forms, and a pop appropriation of an elite form, just as Béla Bartók incorporating Hungarian folk songs into his compositions is an elite appropriation of folk culture. And just to round out the borrowing nicely, the Boston Pops would be an example of elite culture borrowing from pop culture.

This type of cultural appropriation isn't limited to songs, either. TV shows and movies (and sometimes even the news) love using urban legends, folktales, and current jokes; and folk culture steals narrative content from pop culture in return. There are tons of people out in the world saying the phrase "May the force be with you," not because they're big fans of *Star Wars*, but simply because their friends keep saying it. So again, while these categories are illustrative, they're definitely not airtight.

It should be clear by now that defining folklore is as much about understanding how it moves as understanding what it is. Folklore is a part of informal[12] culture, it moves via word of mouth and observation, rather than by formal or institutional means. And as we discussed earlier, what this means is that the lore, the stuff that's being passed around (which could be stories, customs, beliefs, whatever) isn't limited to a single correct version. When a cultural expression is (re)created anew each time it gets shared, it varies a bit, and it's this variation that allows us to identify a particular cultural form as folklore. Got that? Variation is the marker that we look for when trying to identify the folk process.

Here's an example: let's say that you write a great story and publish it in the school newspaper. You grab a bunch of copies of the paper to give your friends, and you e-mail the e-edition of the paper to your family. Let's say the Associated Press eventually picks up your story (wow—you're clearly a great writer!). Suddenly your story is running in the *New York Times,* the *Los Angeles Times,* and other impressive newspapers. If you gathered up all those different versions of your story and compared them side by side, they'd all be identical. That's because, of course, they were transmitted via mass media—they'd all be attributed to you, and they'd all have the same exact content.

Now let's change the situation: say you hear a neat story from a friend and tell it to another friend. The person you told it to then turns around and tells it to some more people. Those people, however, don't know the person the story was originally about, so some of the details that only a good friend would care about get dropped. One of those people then decides to type up the story to e-mail it to a sibling who lives far away. The sibling then e-mails it to some more people, maybe adding a few sentences to the top of the e-mail to explain where it came from and the reason for forwarding it. Then those people forward it on, too, but they may erase the explanation that the e-mail came with, and they'll probably also erase the list of previous recipients at the top of the e-mail just to save space, so the identity of the person who first typed it up is lost. Maybe one of the next recipients is a grammar fanatic who goes in and rewrites some of the more awkward sentences before forwarding it on again. A few more steps down the line, maybe someone else changes the city the story takes place in, so that it's more relatable to the people she plans to forward it on to. Perhaps some of those recipients don't really like burdening their friends with e-mail forwards so they don't forward it on, but it's such a good story that it ends up being told at a dinner party or around the water cooler or while just hanging out. Now, if you held all those different versions of your story side by side, they'd be different—folklorists would say that they "exhibit dynamic variation." Without ever talking to you, a folklorist could determine that your story had been transmitted via the folk process, rather than via mass media, by recognizing the variation. This is one way we identify folklore.

Variation also implies another important marker of folklore: there has to be more than one version of something in order for it to vary. So in order to identify something as folklore, we have to find it in more than one place. Let's say that you write down a story in your secret journal that you never let anyone read. Even if it sounds like a folktale (with princesses and witches and fairy godmothers and magic mirrors) or sounds like an urban legend (with hook-handed maniacs and persecuted babysitters), it's not folklore until it's been passed along. Remember, identifying folklore is all about identifying how it travels; if it hasn't traveled at all, then it's simply not folklore.[13] In fact, if it hasn't been shared, it's simply not "folk"—remember, "folk" implies "culture," which implies "group," not a single person. This is why we so often call folklore "traditional"—it gets passed on from person to person, leaving multiple versions in its wake.

This isn't exactly the way that most people use the word *traditional*.[14] Sure, the idea that traditional means "passed on" makes sense given the fact that we commonly think of traditions as coming to us from the past. A meal you've prepared is traditional if your great-grandparents cooked it, too. A holiday custom is traditional if that's the way it was done in the old country. A ballad is traditional if it was composed thousands of years ago. In the study of folklore, however, it's important to note that calling something "traditional" doesn't mean it's "old." A brand-new legend or rumor can be passed along via e-mail to thousands of people in just a few days—*and that's still traditional*. Traditional simply means passed on, whether that's over many generations or over just a few days, resulting in the same expressive form cropping up in multiple places.

Let's put these two ideas together. Folk transmission is informal, and so one identifier of folklore is variation. And folklore is traditional, so another identifier of folklore is that it's passed on.

At long last we have boiled it down to some basic rules we can follow when identifying folklore: folklore is informal (meaning variable) and traditional (meaning passed on). Folklorist Barre Toelken used the words "dynamic" and "conservative" to express the same idea.[15] Dynamic means variable; conservative means traditional. If we were to watch a piece of folklore travel through a population, we would be able to identify the dynamic elements as the details that change with each new telling, that reflect the unique contexts in which the folklore is shared. We would be able to identify the conservative elements as the parts that stay the same, that tell us we're still looking at the "same" piece of folklore, despite the variation. To identify a cultural form—a story, joke, custom, or anything, really—as folklore, we want to seek these two basic qualities: it's folklore if it's passed on via person-to-person transmission, creating multiple versions in which we recognize conservative elements (that is, it's traditional), and if those multiple versions are dynamic and variable, with details changing to fit new contexts and new tellers, so that there's no single right version (that is, it's informal).

So finally, many pages later, we have reached our answer: folklore is informal, traditional culture. Those three words are our shorthand for the whole general mish-mash of what folklore is. In those

three words we are reminded of the importance of both halves of
the word folk-lore: without the folk (people sharing an informal
culture) we wouldn't have dynamic variation, and without the lore
(the stories, beliefs, and customs), we wouldn't have anything to
pass on traditionally. It's a big concept in a small package.

SO WHAT?

The definition of folklore as "informal traditional culture" is much
broader than many people initially expect, and it also helps to work
against the common misperception that folklore has to be old (and
rural, backward, and untrue). For a long time, back when folklorists thought the "folk" were peasants, folklorists thought that all
folklore was slowly disappearing from the world as peasant populations were becoming more educated and economically independ-
ent. The conception of folklore as informal traditional culture,
however, highlights that folklore is always coming into and falling
out of use. A particular item of folklore may indeed disappear if it's
no longer relevant to people's lives, but folklore on the whole will
never disappear—we'll always have informal, traditional aspects to
our cultural lives.[16]

This is a pretty uplifting message, if you think about it. We've
got a lot going on in the realm of culture these days—globalization,
McDonaldization, homogenization, digitization, depersonaliza-
tion—lots of -izations that make people worry about the cultural,
expressive, and interpersonal future of the human race. To be sure,
folklore isn't all butterflies and rainbows—it includes racist, sexist,
xenophobic, and vulgar content as often as not[17]—but the contin-
ued existence of folklore does have some good news to offer. Even
if some aspects of our society are homogenizing, or even if some
aspects of our interpersonal communication are being stripped
of spontaneity and individuality, there's always going to be a folk
realm where shared, emergent, discursive, and expressive culture is
growing and developing. Even in the most dry and scripted of corporate environments, folk culture exists—always has, always will.
And studying it will help us gain a more balanced understanding of
life, the universe, and everything.

Now, I realize that those are some big claims for a little discipline, but I stand by them. The study of a group's folklore can often reveal the heart and soul of that group in a way that focusing on other aspects can't. Folklorists have long noted what they call the "triviality barrier"[18] in the field of folklore studies. Because people's own folklore is so common, so familiar, so everyday, many people feel that it's not worth studying. Now, if we look to the folklore of other cultures, it may indeed seem exotic and strange, but it's important to remember that folklore isn't defined by being exotic and strange; it only looks that way from the outside. To the people who grew up in that other culture, that same exotic and strange folklore appears mundane and familiar.

But there's a strong argument to be made in favor of studying the mundane, the familiar, and the trivial, and we can see it when we look at the root of the word *trivia*.[19] It comes to us from the Latin *trivium*, which means "three roads" or, specifically, the spot where three roads come together. Like this:

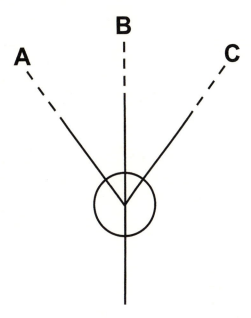

Fig. 1.4

Now, let's say you were going to build a marketplace for people from towns A, B, and C to visit. Where is the most likely place to put that market? At the trivium, of course, the place that is most relevant to all three of those populations. Seeking cultural understanding is a similar endeavor. If we want to understand a group of people—not individuals, but the group as a whole—we need to look at the things they share, the places where their lives intersect, rather than at the things that distinguish them. In other words, we can learn a lot about the Irish people by reading the works of James Joyce, as he was an insightful man who had a way with words, but when we read his books, we're also learning a whole lot about James Joyce as an individual. If we look to the folklore—the customs, stories, beliefs, and so on—that's been shared, promoted, and shaped by the Irish people as a whole, we're going to have a much better understanding of that group.[20] The commonness of folklore is exactly what makes it so important as a subject of cultural study.

So, what are we left with, here? Are you ready to show up at a party and field the "What is folklore?" question that inevitably arises when you reveal that you're taking a folklore class? It's okay if the answer is no—any folklore grad student can tell you that it sometimes takes years to get to a point where you're comfortable explaining the discipline to others on the fly. For now, here's a helpful script. You can carry it around with you to read to people when they ask.[21]

> Folklore is informal, traditional culture. It's all the cultural stuff—customs, stories, jokes, art—that we learn from each other, by word of mouth or observation, rather than through formal institutions like school or the media. Just as literature majors study novels and poems or art historians study classic works of art, folklorists focus on the informal and traditional stuff, like urban legends and latrinalia.

WANT TO KNOW MORE?

Barre Toelken, *The Dynamics of Folklore* (Logan: Utah State University Press, 1996).

Toelken presents a readable and informative introduction to the study of folklore, offering lots of case studies that allow for learning about the traditions themselves as well as how to approach and analyze them. Examples from Toelken's experiences with the Navajo culture make this a great book for anyone interested in Native American culture.

Martha Sims and Martine Stephens, *Living Folklore: An Introduction to the Study of People and Their Traditions* (Logan: Utah State University Press, 2005).

This book covers a lot of those complex, ambiguous, theoretical ideas of the field and presents them in a way that helps them make sense. It doesn't skimp on the detail, making it an excellent choice if you're looking to go beyond a basic introduction to folklore.

Alan Dundes, *The Study of Folklore* (Englewood Cliffs, NJ: Prentice Hall, 1965).

And oldie but goodie. Dundes has influenced several generations of folklorists with his straightforward assertions about the field, and while any of his works come with a touch of his favorite method of analysis—psychoanalysis—his ability to encompass the subject of folklore clearly and concisely can't be beat.

Elliott Oring, *Folk Groups and Folklore Genres: An Introduction* (Logan: Utah State University Press, 1986).

Oring brings together a number of folklorists, each of whom provides a chapter on his or her own area of expertise, while Oring himself introduces the subject nicely, highlighting the need for identification of the common denominators that unite all things folk. There is a reader that accompanies this text for those who want even more elaboration and backstory on the concepts at hand.

NOTES

1. On August 22, no less, which I declare to be International Folklore Day from now on. William Thoms, "Folk-lore and the Origin of the Word," in *International Folkloristics*, ed. Alan Dundes (Lanham, MD: Rowman and Littlefield, 1999), 9–14.

2. It's a bit confusing, but "folklore" is both the name of the academic field and the stuff that people in that field study. There have been many debates over the years about changing the name to something more scholarly and impressive (like "cultural studies" or "verbal art" or "ethnology"), but folklore just seems to stick. Occasionally you'll see the phrase "folklore studies," which this book uses, or "folkloristics," which folklorists use when they want to seem more impressive.

3. There's actually a technical term for bathroom graffiti: *latrinalia*. It's a fun idea to try to work this word into as many college essays as possible.

4. Interestingly, many of the most famous definitions of folklore can be boiled down to this two-part concept. Possibly the most commonly taught definition of

folklore is Dan Ben-Amos's "artistic communication in small groups," and we can see that "artistic communication" is basically "lore" and "small groups" is basically the "folk." Dan Ben-Amos, "Toward a Definition of Folklore in Context," *Journal of American Folklore* 84 (January–March 1971): 3–15.

5. Ward Goodenough, *Cultural Anthropology and Linguistics*, Report of the Seventh Annual Round Table Meeting on Linguistics and Language Study, ed. Paul L. Garvin, Monograph Series on Languages and Linguistics 9 (Washington, DC: Georgetown University Press, 1957).

6. Alan Dundes, *The Study of Folklore* (Englewood Cliffs, NJ: Prentice Hall, 1965), 2.

7. Or even just two members: think about all the inside jokes and coded words that couples or siblings share—nicknames, single words that reference entire experiences, coded gestures to let the other person know you need to be rescued from an awkward conversation at a party, etc.

8. I should point out that the word "informal" here doesn't mean "casual" or "laid-back" "unimportant," it simply means that it's not dictated by an institution.

9. I don't want to encourage the misperception that folklore is only stories, or narrative forms, here, but it's helpful at this point to have a single, familiar example to consider. There are a lot more forms of folklore than just stories, including some entirely nonverbal forms of folklore like hand gestures and material objects; if you find that the ideas in the upcoming section make sense with the story example, consider trying them out with a folk gesture or folk custom example.

10. Even more interesting is the situation in which I tell a joke poorly, and you turn around and tell it the right way. Because folklore is variable, it can be self-correcting—we don't have to live with unsuccessful versions of folklore, we just make them better as we pass them on!

11. With some forms of folklore, especially folk songs, the original author is sometimes known, or at least can be discovered through research, but in the folk process that identification is often stripped out quickly.

12. Again, this just means noninstitutionally dictated. Calling folk culture "informal" *doesn't* mean that folklore is necessarily casual or insignificant or unimportant. It simply means that folklore isn't distributed via a publishing house or protected by copyright or enforced by the government, and thus is free to evolve, adapt, and be adjusted to different tellers and audiences.

13. Yet. It may certainly become folklore later, if it eventually gets passed around a lot.

14. Get used to this: folklorists love to use familiar words in specialized ways.

15. Barre Toelken, *The Dynamics of Folklore* (Logan: Utah State University Press, 1996).

16. Just a quick note on the grammar of folklore: "folklore" is a mass noun, not a count noun. What does that mean? It means that grammatically, "folklore" is the same as "butter" or "milk" or any other (dairy or nondairy) noun that isn't by itself countable. For example, you wouldn't say, "I have five butters"; you'd say, "I have five pats of butter." You wouldn't say, "I drank three milks"; you'd say, "I drank three glasses of milk." This is because pats and glasses are count nouns, while

butter and milk are mass nouns. Similarly, you would never say, "I collected seven folklores today"; you'd say, "I collected seven pieces of folklore today" or simply, "I collected seven legends today." In addition, "folklore" isn't an adjective; "folk" is. So if you want to explain that a story you've discovered exhibits the qualities of folklore, you'd say that it's a "folk story," not a "folklore story." You have no idea how many people make these mistakes, and you have no idea how silly they sound to folklorists when they do. Don't make these mistakes. Don't sound silly.

17. Many folklore course syllabi include some kind of warning about this: folklore reveals a culture as it is, not as we would wish it to be. Ignoring the unpleasant parts leaves us with an incomplete and less than useful understanding. The study of folklore can lead to some surprisingly explicit discussions, so it's good to be prepared. I doubt your instructors will expect you to enjoy or approve of it, but any folklore student should be prepared to consider disturbing or questionable content academically.

18. Brian Sutton-Smith used this term to talk about the scholarly disregard for children's folklore in particular. "Psychology of Childlore: The Triviality Barrier," *Western Folklore* 29 (January 1970): 1–8.

19. Elliott Oring describes this in detail in his book *Just Folklore* (Long Beach, CA: Cantilever, 2012), chapter 18.

20. And this, of course, goes for any group we might want to understand better: ethnicities, families, occupations, friend circles, political parties, anyone. There's even a recent interest in studying the folklore of corporations and office workers as a beneficial human resources practice.

21. I used to do this. Seriously, it helps.

Chapter 2

What Do Folklorists Do?

So, now you know what folklore is.[1] Pretty neat, huh? There's one more basic question to answer, though, before we start getting into some examples of folklore, and that's what, exactly, do folklorists do when they study folklore? Just as many people have a vague and often incomplete sense of what folklore is, many people are similarly unclear as to what the work of a folklorist entails. It's important to know, though, especially if you decide to major in it and have to justify not getting a business degree to your family and friends.

Let me speak from experience: It's pretty common that at parties and gatherings, when people learn I'm a folklorist, someone will turn to me and say, "Tell us a story!" Ask any folklorist—I guarantee that this has happened at least once to all of us. Since people apparently have some idea that folklore and storytelling go hand in hand, it makes sense that a professional folklorist would be good at telling stories, right?

Well, to be honest, while I certainly do participate in my fair share of folk culture (as do we all), I'm not a particularly captivating storyteller when put on the spot. I, like a lot of people, don't have a repertoire of rehearsed stories at my immediate disposal that would really be what the "Tell us a story!" crowd is looking for. There are certainly a lot of folklorists who are great storytellers, but studying folklore doesn't make you one.

This common misunderstanding, while awkward at parties, does, however, help to highlight some distinctions. I study folklore; I don't necessarily perform folklore. This is the case with scholars in

DOI: 10.7330/9780874219067.c002

many academic fields; in response to a recent "Tell us a story!" scenario, I tried pointing out to the party guests that no one ever asks my criminologist husband to "Commit us a crime!" Unfortunately, while I was patting myself on the back for finding such an apt analogy, most of the guests found it a pretty hilarious joke (and still wanted me to tell that story).

But the thing is, it *is* an apt analogy, one that can help people unfamiliar with the field better understand what is it that folklorists do. Crime is a component of culture; it emerges from within a society or group of people. So does folklore, as we discussed in the previous chapter. Criminologists study crime, the different types of crime that crop up in different cultures, the social and psychological influences that encourage or discourage those crimes, and so on, just as folklorists study folklore, the different kinds of folklore that crop up in different cultures, the social and psychological influences that shape and promote the sharing of that folklore, and so on. If only there were as many prime-time dramas about folklore as there are about crime, we folklorists might not have to go around finding apt analogies all the time.

So, folklorists don't necessarily perform the folklore they study, at least not as a part of their professional work as folklorists, any more than criminologists commit the crimes they study.[2] Sure, folklorists will probably learn lots of songs and customs and stories during their formal education, and if there's the inclination and talent, it just might turn into a distinct skill set,[3] but that's separate from their work as folklorists.

The crime analogy only goes so far, of course; for one, folklore is often seen as a positive thing to emerge from a community (though we know this is not always the case, as folklore can be nasty, vulgar, and cruel as often as it can be beautiful and inspiring), so while criminologists are often focused on preventing the growth of crime, folklorists are often engaged in encouraging or admiring (or at least not trying to prohibit) the growth of folklore.

But stick with me—the analogy can take us a bit further. Just as some professionals in the field of criminology decide to focus on applying their knowledge about crime to practical uses in a community (say, by becoming a police officer or an FBI profiler), some professional folklorists decide similarly to focus on the applied side of folklore studies. They take their understanding of folklore and apply it within their communities by creating archives and museum exhibits to preserve and display information about local cultures for educational, documentary, and entertainment purposes, or by serving as cultural mediators in fields like international business or medicine.[4]

On the other hand, some scholars who study crime decide to focus on the more theoretical aspects of the issue—considering what causes crime, what factors influence who commits a crime and who doesn't, or what blend of individual and environment creates a potential criminal. Some folklorists similarly choose to focus on more theoretical questions about folklore—determining how we distinguish one genre from another, how a particular piece of folklore functions in a community, or what a certain tradition expresses or reflects for the group that shares it.

From these two approaches, which certainly aren't wholly separate from each other, we get the two main types of professional folklore work: public folklore and academic folklore. Much has been made over the years of this dichotomy, the split between public and academic folklorists, and you can read articles or talk to folklorists about both the distressing divisiveness and the beneficial cooperation between these two types of work. The reality is that they both take a bit from each other, and choosing one over the other as an area of focus usually has more to do with whether you want to work in the public sector or at a university than with what you want to do or not do (or think or not think) as a folklorist.

This book, however, is designed to tell you about the academic field of folklore studies, so that's what we're going to focus on here. If public folklore is of interest to you, I encourage you to find yourself some public folklorists and start pestering them with questions. For now, let's discuss what academic folklorists do.

Well, for starters, folklorists collect folklore. That's nice and straightforward, isn't it? While the collection of folklore used to be considered an end in itself, that's not really the case anymore. As I mentioned in the last chapter, for quite some time (think early to mid-1800s until fairly recently), the general assumption among folklorists (who were usually identified, at that time, as either anthropologists or antiquarians) was that folklore was disappearing. They saw folklore as this glorious beacon of the noble past that was slowly but surely slipping away.[5]

This, of course, was tied closely to the idea that the "folk" were a limited segment of society—the poor, the illiterate, the uneducated. Scholars believed that folklore was the leftovers of an earlier age, leftovers that likely contained important remnants of a culture that the elite and educated classes were sadly yet inevitably leaving behind, leftovers that needed to be rescued from imminent demise.

We, of course, know better now. Everyone is the folk; everyone lives cultural lives on both formal (institutional) and informal (folk) levels. Rather than seeing folklore as something that's slipping away, we now recognize it as something that ebbs and flows with the times. Folklore has no institutional anchor; the minute it's no longer relevant to us, it's gone. Sure, collecting it and lovingly storing it in an archive is probably a good idea in case it never crops up again, but what, exactly, are we saving it for?

Thus we come to the second, and far more important, job of a folklorist: analysis. Folklore studies is an analytical field, just like anthropology and literary studies, the two fields from which it derives most of its tools and methods. Like anthropologists, folklorists examine and consider the behavior that surrounds folklore, the processes by which folklore is learned and shared, and thus the process through which it varies and evolves. Like literary scholars, folklorists also examine and consider the folklore itself (the texts of narratives, certainly, but also objects, rituals, concepts, and customs), and look for meaning and patterns in the content. These two approaches, looking at the text and at the context, lay the foundation for the study of folklore.

COLLECTING FOLKLORE

You have an assignment: go out and collect some folklore. Sounds easy enough, right? Gather your friends, maybe bribe them with food, ask them to tell you some jokes or stories or to describe what their families do at the holidays, and you're good. Right?

Well, here's the thing: there's a whole lot going on when folklore emerges naturally through interaction that can't be captured simply by writing down the words of a story or joke (or taking a picture of a quilt or describing a holiday custom). For one thing, the words or actions that make up a folk narrative or a traditional behavior don't exist in a vacuum. The general cultural and social setting in which the folklore is being performed affect both the form and the reception of the folklore. Jokes that are thigh-slappingly hilarious in one country don't always translate humorously in another; the cultural background for folklore always needs to be noted.

There's also the more immediate setting in which the folklore happens—where and when it is performed,[6] and who's there listening or watching. If you don't think this affects how folklore is presented, think of what happens when someone is telling a dirty joke and their parents—or their children—walk into the room. Suddenly that joke isn't so dirty anymore (or suddenly there's no joke being told at all!). If someone were to read only the words of that joke, the sudden switch in tone or language wouldn't make sense without an explanation of the sudden change in audience.

And keep in mind, while it's ideal to imagine yourself encountering folklore in its natural habitat, ready with your phone's voice recorder app to capture your friends' natural banter as it occurs, it's unlikely that this is always how you'll get to collect folklore. Let's be realistic: if you're collecting folklore for a class, you're likely calling up your family two days before your whole project is due and asking them to please tell you some of those funny stories they always tell at Thanksgiving dinner, so you can record and transcribe them.

This usually results in less than natural settings for the collection of folklore. So it's important to find out how the setting of collection differs from the setting in which the folklore would usually appear, because the folklore might be altered because of it. For example, that dirty joke's punch line might still be told, but in a whisper rather than a shout, depending on who's around when you finally get your friend to tell it.

This brings up yet another issue—not simply *where* and *when* the folklore is shared, but *how* it is shared. Is the story told or the song sung in a lively way or a somber way? Is the recipe made casually, with imprecise measurements, or painstakingly, with per-fectly leveled scoops? Is the celebration carried out identically each time, rehearsed down to the minute, or does it not really matter if things are replicated perfectly? Is the joke told as if it is truly funny, or as if it's not funny at all? Is the punch line whispered or shouted? These are the questions that keep folklorists up at night, as these are often the questions that lead to an understanding of the folklore on a deeper level.

Folklorists have come up with numerous ways to deal with all this necessary extra info when collecting folklore. Different archives have different formats in which they like to have information sub-mitted, but in general, there are some guidelines that are accepted across the board. Folklorist Alan Dundes[7] came up with the three-part consideration of text, context, and texture as the main things to make note of when collecting folklore. In brief, the text is the what; the context is the where, the when, and the who (or the with whom, to be more grammatically precise); and the texture is the how.

So, to put it in practical terms of what you would need to con-sider when collecting, say, a joke, you'd want to know what the joke is (the text, often summed up as "the thing itself"—the words of the joke, in this case, and a description of any integral gestures or expressions); where, when, and with whom the joke would normally be performed (the context, on several levels—the general cultural context as well as the more specific contexts of use and collection); and how the joke is normally performed (the texture—the tone, pitch, volume, rhythm, rhyme, and general attitude of the joke).

Filling in these three categories of information can be accom-plished in different ways. Folklorists generally refer to the process of going out and conducting interviews and such as "fieldwork," and this is the most common method of gathering information. It's important to note that folkloristic interviews aren't your typical nightly news, back-and-forth, information-gathering interviews. Folklore is an emergent conversational form of communication, so we want to re-create that kind of setting when collecting folklore.

Visit with your informant[8] somewhere comfortable and casual. Leave the recorder on the table so you're not holding it in your infor-mant's face. Get your informants talking, rather than bombarding them with questions right off the bat. In fact, maybe even share a bit of your own folklore to give them a sense of what you're looking for. Of course, some collection projects (those involving music, for example, or dance) can require more involved and technical setups for recording, and there are whole manuals written about the minutiae of fieldwork, but in general, when collecting folklore, think of creating the kind of environment where folklore would naturally flourish, and go from there.

Of course, these days, fieldwork is as often accomplished online—via e-mail, chat, Facebook, or Skype—as it is in person. This is fine. These are all normal, everyday means of communication that we use, and all three kinds of information—text, context, and texture—can be determined through these methods. Sure, texture is different in a chat room than in a face-to-face interview (are they using emoticons, typing fast or slow, spelling carefully or sloppily?), but there's always a way to manage it.

And direct questioning isn't the only way that folklorists get information, either. As anthropologists know, the general practice of "ethnography," or the description of a culture, involves not only interviewing but also observation. As we discussed in chapter 1, folklorists are interested not only in the particular genres of lore, but in folk culture in general. Sitting back and taking in the situation when you're with the people from whom you're collecting folklore can provide a good understanding of the contexts of both use and collection.

Paying attention to the ways people interact, both with each other and with the space they're in, provides lots of opportunities for identifying the unspoken cultural knowledge that people are putting to use in a given situation. The practice of ethnographic observation often involves consideration of both emic (insider) and etic (outsider) perspectives, which can require seeing familiar situations in a new light. We often don't scrutinize our own cultural settings this way (I'm betting you haven't spend a lot of time wondering how everyone in a McDonald's knows not to sit and wait to be served), but it can be a helpful technique to employ when attempting to thoroughly understand the multiple and nuanced contexts of folklore.

Now, this all may sound fairly straightforward, and you can probably imagine yourself easily coaxing folklore from your friends and family—recording their descriptions of traditions, transcribing their stories, noting their gestures and facial expressions as they talk. And sometimes it is that easy. One past student of mine, Anya, had a grandfather who was known in his hometown as a ballad singer and tall-tale teller, and all Anya had to do was sit down with him, ask him to run through a few of his most popular stories and songs (a request he was familiar with, one that many people made of him on a regular basis), and within just a few hours, she had a great set of stories and songs recorded.[9] Of course, she needed to document context and texture, but she could easily do that from memory—she'd spent her whole life listening to her grandfather tell these stories and sing these songs, so documenting the where, when, and how wasn't difficult at all.

Of course, there are some flaws with Anya's approach. Perhaps there are some meaningful stories that aren't among her grandfather's most popular, stories that come out only on certain occasions, or that he wouldn't want to tell in front of his granddaughter. And the contexts and textures that Anya perceives may not be the same as the perceptions of her grandfather or another audience member. The assumption of understanding and familiarity when you're interviewing people you know well can often lead to overlooking some interesting and significant aspects of the folklore you're collecting. Anyone in Anya's situation, easy though the collecting might be, would want to be wary of jumping only to the most apparent or obvious conclusions when analyzing the collected materials.

Let's consider a different collection experience: Craig was a student who wanted to collect folklore from his roommates. Craig knew that his roommates were quite clever and funny, that they had been friends since high school and were always hanging out together telling stories about past parties or crazy stuff they'd done, and he thought he'd be able to get many stories and jokes from them. Specifically, he was thinking of their common pastime of visiting the local Walmart late at night and causing minor havoc amid the aisles—his roommates were always telling stories about run-ins with employees or store security, and he even knew some of the more infamous stories well enough to prompt his friends if they forgot.

To conduct his first interview, Craig arranged to have his roommates and some of their other high school friends visit his dorm. When he initially laid out the topic, "those stories about the stuff you all used to do at Walmart," the group was enthusiastic but a bit unfocused. Lots of references to stories were immediately produced—comments like, "Oh! Like that time Rob rode the tricycle and knocked over the microwaves!" or "Chris's thing about the women's restroom is funny!"—but no actual stories were volunteered. When Craig specifically asked the group to tell the stories, they fell flat: "Well, you've heard it before—that's pretty much it. Rob took a tricycle from the toy department and crashed it into a big endcap stack of microwaves." Craig knew for a fact that he'd heard these guys tell a very long, very funny version of that same story before, but it simply wasn't happening when he tried to collect it.

Craig's friends decided that the best way to help was to visit Walmart together, so Craig unexpectedly found himself crammed in a car, trying to hold his phone up to continue to record the conversation (which wasn't really focused on Walmart stories anymore anyway). At the store, they all got drinks from the Subway restaurant which, they explained to Craig, was how a typical night would start. Of course, it wasn't nighttime when they visited, and there were lots of shoppers around, so the typical antics didn't take place. They wandered around the store a bit, pointing out places where memorable things had happened, and then went home. Craig was left with roughly two hours of very garbled recordings, an empty drink cup, and very few ideas of how to go about picking out stories from the mess of information he'd gathered.

Craig's situation is a very common one on many levels. First off, many people don't see their folklore as folklore, and when the storytelling is taken out of a natural context, it's awkward for most people to go into full detail of a story that they know the person to whom they're talking has already heard. The stories Craig was hoping to collect weren't really folklore in Craig's friends' understanding of the term, and in fact, they didn't really think of them as stories at all—they were just good times, things that had happened that were funny to remember. None of the guys he interviewed would have referred to themselves as "storytellers"—they simply didn't think of themselves and their folk culture in that way.

It's easy to sympathize with Craig's frustrations, but rather than focusing on what Craig didn't get, we need to consider what he did get out of his fieldworking experience. Clearly, Craig's assumptions about what he was looking for were incorrect, or at least incomplete. While he got a few brief stories, he got several other genres as well—customs, foodways, pranks[10]—and more important, he got a wealth of contextual and textural information. As revealing as the short story of the tricycle is, the fact that the guys implicitly knew that daytime was an inappropriate time to engage in mischievous behavior is telling; for as much as they apparently enjoyed hassling the late-night employees, they drew the line at inconveniencing regular shoppers.

Craig got clear information about the appropriate (and inappropriate) where, when, and with whom of this folklore, and also about the how, the attitude behind the traditions. While a second interview was obviously necessary (and was made much more useful through Craig's idea to bring a new person along to provide a fresh audience for the telling of complete stories), the jumbled and confusing trip to Walmart provided Craig with a foundation of understanding for what life in this folk group was really like. In any collecting situation, it's important to set aside expectations and consider what folk culture you're actually getting.

ANALYZING FOLKLORE

Once you've collected your folklore, you're ready to do something with it. One of the best things about the field of folklore studies is that since folklorists are united by what they study, rather than by how they study it, folklorists get to use any and all methods and approaches that seem useful to them. We get to take useful tools from lots of different fields and put them to work for us in whatever way helps us understand our material better.

As we talked about in the previous chapter, folklorists look at folklore as a thing, and also as a process of transmission. We can ask, "What is it?" and also "How does it work?" and "How does it travel?" Jan Harold Brunvand, a folklorist perhaps most famous for his lifelong work with urban legends,[11] put together a list of questions that folklorists commonly ask, and it's a helpful summary.

Folklorists ask questions about:

- definition (what folklore is)
- classification (what the genres of folklore are and how to distinguish between them)
- source (who the "folk" are)
- origin (who originally composed or created folklore)
- transmission (how folklore is carried and how fast and how far)
- variation (how folklore changes and evolves, and for what reasons)
- structure (what the underlying form of folklore is and the relationship of form to content)
- function (what folklore communicates for its carriers and how it works within a group)
- purpose (what the performer intends to convey and the intended effect on the audience)
- meaning (what the folklore may symbolize or represent in a metaphorical way)
- use/application (what the study of folklore can do for other fields and in other areas)[12]

While folklorists examine all these questions, the most common form of study, especially in the sense of analyzing a particular interesting type of folklore that comes from a particular group, is a functional analysis. Answering the question "What does this folklore do for the people who share it?" is a popular academic pursuit for folklorists, especially since there are so many possible answers.

Another famous folklorist, William Bascom, once wrote an article called "The Four Functions of Folklore" in which he claimed that folklore can serve to entertain, to validate a culture's customs and rituals, to teach lessons, and to exercise social control.[13] Are these the only ways that folklore can function? Not remotely. In a broad sense these are certainly applicable to many kinds of folklore, but the smaller the group, the more nuanced the function. Sometimes the folklore of a very small group, such as a single family, serves a unique function that doesn't even exist outside of that group.

I had a student once who grew up in a large family that shared one very small bathroom. Over the years, the family members had developed a whole lexicon of folk speech used to evaluate and compare each other's relative needs to use the facilities—whose case was the most extreme and thus merited first usage, what new situations could override the previously determined order of usage, and so on. The terminology stemmed mainly from funny or embarrassing incidents in the family's history ("This is a 'Julie-in-Yellowstone' situation here!") and was comprehensible and useful only among family members within the family home. The student also felt that the folk speech, which on the surface could appear to be crudely pragmatic, reflected her parents' and siblings' enjoyment of even the downsides of a large family—their insider terminology made them feel closer, provided them with a humorous method to negotiate awkward situations, reinforced their sense of unity as a group, and reminded them of the importance of both equitable sharing and graceful concession in the face of greater need.

So the same piece of folklore can serve multiple functions at once. An urban legend can serve as a warning for a whole community or simply as a psychological release for an anxious individual. A political joke can allow an adult to test the leanings of a social gathering, or it can allow a young person to unofficially push against parental ideology. A folk song can serve as a literal commentary on current or historical events, or as a symbolic expression of complex emotion. A customary holiday game or sporting event can provide social release as well as reinforce a group's identity.

You can probably see already that a research question about function would require a close examination of the folklore itself (the component parts of the custom as practiced, the words of the narrative in its most common variations, the form and feel of the handmade object, etc.), meaning that you'd better have done a great, detailed job documenting and transcribing the folklore you collected (or, if you're getting your folklore from an archive, you'd better hope that whoever collected it did a great job for you).

And of course, such a research question will also require a consideration of the ways in which the folklore emerges from within the group (the common social and cultural contexts, the acceptable—and, sometimes more revealing, the unacceptable—audiences for the folklore, the ways different individuals alter the folklore and their reasons for doing so, etc.), meaning that you really want to have done a bang-up job noting the context and texture along with the text.

Craig's folklore collection experience is a good illustration of this. If we want to consider the function of Craig's roommates' Walmart traditions, it's clear that the text alone won't cut it. If we looked only at the content of the story about Rob riding a tricycle into a stack of microwaves, we might assume that the function of that folklore—whether the custom of behaving that way or the story that is told in remembrance—is to promote an appearance of toughness, destructiveness, or recklessness. If we add in Craig's understanding of the context and texture, however—that the group was conscientious of shoppers' experiences—then we have a more nuanced representation of their values. If we consider that the stated target of their antics was typically the employees, not the customers, then we can perhaps read an anticorporation message into the tradition, rather than a generally antisocial one. We begin to understand something about the culture of these young men in particular, and perhaps the culture of young men in a rural community in general; we learn about the push and pull between impressing one's friends and respecting authorities, and the ways these particular friends express and reinforce their values for each other in their choices of what to remember in story, what to laugh at and what to cringe at, and what activities to engage in at certain times in certain places. A consideration of the text, context, and texture—of the thing itself as well as the behavior that surrounds it—is required for a complete understanding of the folklore.

You may be wondering at this point why on earth anyone would bother to study academically Craig's friends' juvenile Walmart traditions. In the face of more obviously "important" folklore (the collections of the Brothers Grimm, world mythology, native peoples' customs), the antics of some teenagers in a small town seem unimpressive as a form of cultural expression. Well, while we certainly do not want to turn away from studying "important"-seeming folklore, we need to consider the reality of the situation. It would be great if young men in small towns sat around telling each other creation myths, but most don't. If we want to understand the culture of young rural men, we need to look at the folk culture they *actually* have, not the culture we think they *should* have. The folklore we choose to study depends largely on the group of people we're interested in understanding.

SO WHAT?

Before we wrap up this chapter, I want to clarify why folklorists bother to do these things (or, perhaps more significant, why universities would pay folklorists to do these things). Well, one, because it's fun. We shouldn't ignore that fact, though it probably has more to do with individual scholars' choices to study folklore than it does with why a university would value the study of folklore.

The significance of folklore studies as an academic field comes back to the idea that folklore exists as a form of cultural expression without the anchor of institutional culture. Think of it this way: if everyone everywhere slowly came to the conclusion that the works of Charles Dickens were no longer relevant to our society—that the average person had nothing to gain from reading them—would literature students suddenly stop reading them? No. Because the works of Charles Dickens are a part of the official canon, the institutionally recognized collection of what has been determined to be relevant to education.

Here's another example: the law. Perhaps we realize that a particular law is no longer relevant to our society. Well, we can't just decide to start doing it differently—we'd get thrown in jail! As discussed earlier, laws are a part of our formal culture; they require institutional administration in order to be changed, and it takes an awfully long time to change them. Legal changes can be slow to catch up with cultural changes.

Folklore, on the other hand, isn't institutionally determined. That urban legend no longer speaks to something we care about? Gone. That custom no longer meets the needs of that family?

Done—never happens again. While we may record the legend or a description of the custom in an archive so that we remember it was once relevant, there's no formal organization still making us tell the legend or practice the custom. Unlike reading the past works of a famous author or obeying an outdated law, the moment folklore is no longer relevant, we simply stop using it.

What this means, of course (and this is the really important part, so make sure you write it down), is that if folklore is currently circulating, *it must be important.* It certainly may not seem important on the surface—as we know, folklore is often perceived to be trivial—but no one is making that folklore stick around. If it were completely superfluous, totally irrelevant to everyone's lives, it would simply disappear.

So, if we want to understand people, and how people in communities and societies and other groups function and behave and interact (and the longevity of such fields as anthropology, sociology, political science, economics, and marketing suggests we do), then folklore is possibly the single best barometer we have for understanding what is important to a group of people. Sure, we can try to understand a culture by looking at what it teaches through formal education, but students generally learn the stuff they're taught in school because they have to—they're getting tested on it. If we look at the stuff that people in any given group—students, parents, Seventh-Day Adventists, orthodontists, the Irish, whoever—don't have to collectively know but all know anyway, then we're on our way to really understanding them. And that's pretty cool.

WANT TO KNOW MORE?

Bruce Jackson and Edward D. Ives, eds., *The World Observed: Reflections on the Fieldwork Process* (Champaign: University of Illinois Press, 1996).
   Sixteen different scholars (not all strictly folklorists) share their fieldwork experiences in this book, highlighting issues such as ethics, advocacy, identity, and the very human experience of cultural research.
Edward D. Ives, *The Tape-recorded Interview: A Manual for Fieldworkers in Folklore and Oral History* (Knoxville: University of Tennessee Press, 1995).
   I know, I know—who even owns a tape-recorder anymore? But despite the old technology, this short book does a good job of highlighting some of the

social issues of collecting folklore. Ignore the outdated technical stuff and
focus on the situational issues that Ives addresses.

Michael Owen Jones and Robert Georges, *People Studying People: The Human
Element in Fieldwork* (Berkeley and Los Angeles: University of California
Press, 1980).

This book has interdisciplinary applications but is written by folklorists and
speaks to folklorists well. Much more than objective data gathering, fieldwork
is presented as an interpersonal experiment in communication, compromise,
and reflection. The importance of the relationship between folklorist and
informant is highlighted here.

Paddy Bowman and Lynne Hamer, *Through the Schoolhouse Door: Folklore, Community, Curriculum* (Logan: Utah State University Press, 2011).

If you think you're interested in public folklore and want to know more,
this book is a good starting point. While it's mainly focused on education
and ways to incorporate folklore into the classroom, it touches on a number
of themes, including the history of public folklore, various applied folklore
projects, and the perspectives of community members as well as students and
teachers.

NOTES

1. It can be helpful, before moving on to this second chapter, to revisit what
it is you previously thought folklore was before you picked up this book. It can be
hard to overcome preconceived understandings of a common word like folklore,
and comparing what you previously thought to what you know now can be a good
way to avoid falling back into earlier misconceptions. And anyway, rather than
finding out you were wrong, it's possible that you may find out you were right, or
at least partially right. More important, with the basic rules of folklore identification under your belt, you'll know *why* you were right or wrong in your previous
understanding of folklore.

2. Well, we hope they don't.

3. The analogy to crime starts to gets a tad worrisome here.

4. This is just as cool as being a criminal profiler, I promise.

5. Of course, they also felt that the glorious beacons of the past had been cor-
rupted by all those darned peasants, so for a long time there were a lot of entertaining efforts to re-create the original, more impressive forms of things.

6. Don't get hung up on the idea of "performance" as meaning purposefully staged or anything. We're talking about folk performance, which is just the
moments in our normal lives when we switch from daily conversation to telling a
story or joke or to participating in a custom.

7. Alan Dundes is a famous Freudian folklorist; you should read his "Into the
Endzone for a Touchdown: A Psychoanalytic Consideration of American Football," *Western Folklore* 37 (1978): 75–83. He's also the same guy who gave us our
current definition of folk group.

8. This word isn't used here in the FBI, ratting-out-the-mob sense; it simply refers to the person you're interviewing.

9. People like Anya's grandfather, people who are known to be ready with a story, joke, or song, are known as "active bearers" of tradition. Many more people are "passive bearers," people who know the stories, customs, and songs but who don't regularly offer them up or perform them for others. You can collect folklore from both types of tradition bearers, but it's always easier to draw out a passive bearer's knowledge if it's someone you know well. This is a pragmatic thing to keep in mind if you're asked to do a collection project for class.

10. We haven't talked in depth about different genres yet, but take my word for it that these are in there.

11. And his appearances on *Letterman.*

12. Jan Harold Brunvand, *The Study of American Folklore: An Introduction*, 4th ed. (New York: Norton, 1998), 25.

13. William Bascom, "The Four Functions of Folklore," *Journal of American Folklore* 67, no. 266 (1954): 333–49.

Chapter 3

Types of Folklore

Here's what this chapter won't do: this chapter isn't here to give you numerous examples of folklore in the sense of giving you stories to read, customs to try, beliefs to learn about, or anything like that. You can go Google that stuff if you're interested in it, or hit the library and find an interesting collection of folklore to peruse. What this chapter is here to do is tell you about some of the main types of folklore that folklorists have studied and give you one or two cool examples of how each one has been approached or analyzed. Sound boring? It's not.

As I've said in earlier chapters, folklorists study a variety of genres, or types, of folklore. After reading this section, you should be able to identify many of the most common ones and to understand how they're different from each other. What distinguishes a legend from a myth? A calendar custom from a rite of passage? You'll find out!

You'll also discover how the differences in genres can affect the way the folklore functions in society. There are hundreds (if not thousands) of ways to approach each and every genre of folklore, but after reading this section, you'll have at least a few analytical tools in your folklorist tool belt right off the bat. If nothing else, you'll come away with some solid examples of what a close examination of different types of folklore can reveal.

While there are more genres of folklore than can possibly be listed in one place, one easy way to divide them initially is into these four basic categories:

DOI: 10.7330/9780874219067.c003

things we say (like jokes, songs, folktales, myths, and
   legends)
things we do (like calendar customs, rituals, games, and
   rites of passage)
things we make (like handmade objects, collections and
   assemblages, and folk art)
things we believe (like superstitions, supernatural creatures, and folk religion)[1]

It's probably already obvious that there's a good deal of overlap here, especially when it comes to the things we believe. For
example, a legend is something we say about something we believe;
a friendship bracelet is something we make that reflects something
we believe, and a rite of passage is something we do to indicate
something we believe. But as with all the not-so-clear-cut divisions
we've made so far, this one is a useful tool for conceptualizing the
breakdown of folklore, even if it's an oversimplification.

This chapter is going to walk through these four main categories of folklore, describing the main identifying characteristics of
each and offering some initial examples of analysis.[2] Unfortunately
(or fortunately, depending on how tired of reading you are at this
point), there's not enough space in this short handbook to address
all (or even most) of the subtypes included in each general category
of folklore. Instead, each section below will focus on one or two
major genres of folklore within that category, as an illustration of
the possibilities.

THINGS WE SAY

The category of things we say encompasses all the folklore that
comes out of our mouths or through our fingertips and onto a piece
of paper or a screen. That means jokes, slang, proverbs, riddles,
mnemonic devices, rhymes, songs, oaths, toasts, greetings, leave-
takings—basically tons and tons of forms of folklore—but the
most famous, the most well-known, and the most studied forms of
verbal folklore are stories.[3]

It's probably not something you've ever thought about consciously, but there is a big difference between beginning a story with

"Once upon a time . . ." and beginning a story with "You'll never believe what happened to my aunt's hairdresser's cousin's roommate last week!" The main difference is in how we expect our listeners to react to the story we're about to tell, and this is an excellent illustration of how important the distinction between genres is in the realm of folk narrative. When it comes to things we say, folklorists have mainly studied the longer forms of folklore: the legend, the folktale, and the myth.[4]

You probably can already guess that it's a folktale that begins with "Once upon a time," and a legend[5] that begins with the friend-of-a-friend connection.[6] So, what's the difference? Well, for one, no one tells a folktale as though it actually happened. "Once upon a time, in a land far, far away" clearly sets a story in an imaginary place. Thus, when we hear that something amazing or miraculous happens in the story, we don't really have cause to doubt it—it's fiction!

For example, when someone says to you, "Once upon a time, in a land far, far away, there was a cat named Puss who wore a lovely pair of boots and went around making farmers into kings,"[7] you're not expected to react by saying, "Wait. Hold on a sec. Are you honestly telling me that this cat could talk, much less wear human footwear?" By framing this story as a folktale, or as a fictional story, the teller makes it clear that we're supposed to just accept what is happening without question.

On the other hand, if a friend turns to you and says, "You'll never believe what I just heard! My mom's coworker's stepson just got this new pet cat and when he got it home it started trying on his shoes and offering to help him get a promotion at work!" we absolutely would be expected to respond with disbelief.

This illustrates one of the great distinctions between these two types of folk narrative: folktales are told as fiction and set in a fictional world, while legends are told as true[8] and are set in the real world. A story told as fiction is entertainment, perhaps escapism for most people; a story told as true is more of a commentary on contemporary life. This gets at the function of these different types of folklore: legends tend to highlight the stuff that we as a society are stressed out about; folktales tend to help us forget all that for a time.

So, if you were a folklorist out collecting stories, it would be imperative to understand whether you were collecting a folktale or a legend, especially since the content of the story might be the same in both (something strange or unexpected, like talking cats). Let's say you collected a story about someone dining at a fast-food restaurant and making the horrible discovery that what he thought was a piece of chicken was actually a rat. If that story were told as taking place "once upon a time," then it wouldn't have much of a direct societal impact—who cares if some fictional person ate something gross? We might see symbolic metaphors in such a story but, as with most fairytale content, we wouldn't expect the story's content to directly impact our lives.

But if that story is told as *true*, as having happened to someone who knows someone you know, someone very similar to yourself, perhaps, maybe living very close to you (and eating at the same restaurants—oh, horror!), then suddenly that story is saying something more. It's a direct warning about personal health and well-being, it's a public condemnation of a particular business, and it's a social commentary on the conditions of modern food production and consumption. The meaning of that particular story is very dependent on what *type* of folk narrative it is.

So, we have folktales as fiction and legends as true (though not necessarily believed); what about myths? Like legends, myths are told as true, but it's a different kind of truth: it's a sacred truth. Far from the popular use of the word *myth* to mean "something not true," folklorists use this word to refer to a sacred narrative. Sacred to whom, you might ask? Well, to whatever folk group regularly shares it. Calling a particular story a myth is making no claim on the factual reality of that story; it's simply saying that for the people who share it, the story articulates a sacred (or at least fundamental) truth. Myths, like legends, are set in the real world, but often take place in an earlier version of it—our world as it was coming into being—so that, similar to folktales, we aren't intended to readily question the strange or amazing things that we hear in myths. So where we might see strange or miraculous events described here, just as in a folktale or a legend, again, the meaning of the story is unique to the type of narrative. In a myth, we're looking at deeply held, fundamental beliefs of a people.

So, in summary, we have folktales, which are told as fiction, set in a fictional world, and which are only symbolically true, if presented or perceived as true at all. We have legends, which are told as literally true (though not necessarily believed), and set in the real world. And we have myths, which are told as a sacred truth, and which are set in a sort of prototype of our world. As you can see, knowing which genre you're dealing with when you come across a story is enormously helpful when it comes to analyzing the meaning and function of that folk narrative.

Imagine that you're visiting with a friend's family, and during a discussion of the family's immigration to the United States, your friend's mother interrupts to say, "You know, back when great-grandma was a little girl in Sweden, she once saw a *jätte* in the forest." Further explanation reveals that a jätte is a giant, and that your informant's family regularly tells the story of their ancestor's sighting of one with pride. The mother's language tells you that this is a legend—the story is pitched as historical, taking place in the past but in the knowable past, not an ambiguous past of "long, long ago," and in a particular place, Sweden, rather than "a land far, far away." When you ask if the story is true, however, your informants demure, saying that they don't know for sure, that it's always been told that way in the family, that it's maybe possible, because things like that happened in the past, but they can't be certain.

Consider what you know about the context of this telling of the story—it came up right as discussion was turning to the time when the family left Sweden for America, and it brought the conversation back to the topic of Swedish culture. Your friend's family evinces a clear pride in their heritage, and you learn through discussion that the sighting of a jätte is a special thing—it's a marker of genuinely being a Swede. You get the distinct impression that your friend's mother *wants* her great-grandmother to have seen a jätte, to have this uniquely Swedish experience be a part of her family history. It's not enough to simply tell the story abstractly, or to have heard about the jätte; the use of the legend genre ties it to the family's reality in a way that clearly matters to the family's perception and presentation of its own identity. The genre of the narrative clearly supports the story's function within the folk group.

Interestingly, we see the different types of folk narrative rise and fall in popularity over time.[9] Currently, legends are the most actively circulating form of narrative folklore.[10] We rarely encounter folktales or myths in oral form—they tend to come to us in print. What does this mean for these stories? Are they still folklore if they're printed in books?

Yes, they're certainly still folklore, but since folklore is so largely defined by its *process*, they can't really be considered *living* folklore—they're more like a record of once-living folklore. Think of it this way: when an archaeologist digs up an arrowhead and puts it in a museum, is it still an arrowhead? Sure. But to be in its most genuine context of use, that arrowhead should really be at the tip of an arrow, aimed at an animal during a hunt, or in a toolmaker's hands, being carefully shaped and honed. We can learn a lot about the arrowhead by looking at it in the museum, but we're missing a major aspect of its true cultural existence as an object, an aspect we can only guess at or imagine from the museum display. We're also left to wonder if this arrowhead is representative of all arrowheads. Was it made using a common technique or one unique to a particular toolmaker? We would be hesitant to consider this one arrowhead as representative of all arrowheads, or of a whole group of people who used arrowheads, without knowing the ways that it was similar to or different from other arrowheads.

Another good analogy is the study of a dead bee pinned to a card. We can learn an enormous amount about that bee: the structure and systems of its body, its size, shape, form, color, and so on. And if we had lots of bees to look at, we could get a sense of the general range of these qualities—what's considered "typical" of bee form and physiology. But what we don't learn a whole lot about is flight. And how can we really say that we fully understand bees if we don't watch them fly?

This true for stories, too. Just as with the bees and arrowheads, we can learn a whole lot about a folktale or a myth or a legend by examining printed texts. We can scrutinize a single printed version of a story. Ideally, we'll be able to compare many versions (assuming we have many printed versions) of a story side by side and learn the breadth of variation in form, length, content, and so on. We can study the structure of the story: the dynamic qualities that change and the conservative qualities that remain consistent. But to truly understand a folk narrative, we have to watch it fly. We have to be there when it's told so we can observe the teller and the listeners; we have to pay attention to the reactions of the audience and the actions of the performer. Only then can we truly grasp the full picture of a folk narrative.[11]

This is why many folklorists prefer to study contemporary, actively circulating folklore rather than the folklore of the past; it's easier to get the full picture. But of course, this isn't always possible—sometimes the folklore that one wants to study simply isn't actively circulating anymore. Ideally, even if a piece of folklore isn't in active use, the folklorist who documented it will have used the techniques we discussed in chapter 2—documenting not only the text but the context and texture as well, so that future researchers could approximate the experience of watching the bee in flight. Unfortunately, that concentrated focus on context and texture is somewhat new, and not many folklorists of the past took the time to document those details. That doesn't mean that the folklore isn't worth studying—no archaeologist would say that we might as well give up studying arrowheads just because we can't go back in time to watch them in use—but it means that we're limited in how far our contextual analysis can go.

Want to Know More?

William Bascom, "The Forms of Folklore: Prose Narratives," *Journal of American Folklore* 78 (January–March 1965): 3–20.

This is the quintessential article that delineates the differences between folk narrative types, and here's where you'll find a full elaboration of the distinguishing characteristics of folktales, legends, and myths.

Kirin Narayan, *Mondays on the Dark Night of the Moon: Himalayan Foothill Folktales* (New York: Oxford University Press, 1997).

This is a collection of folktales from the Himalayan foothills, presented alongside ethnographic descriptions of the contexts within which they were collected. This is a great attempt to get away from the bee-on-a-card type of story collection; it really works at describing flight as well. Readers get to know the stories, but they get to know the teller and the collector, too, and better understand their relationship with each other and with the stories.

Jan Harold Brunvand, *Too Good to Be True: The Colossal Book of Urban Legends* (New York: Norton, 2001).

Jan Brunvand has written a number of books about urban legends, and any
one of them makes for a fun read. This one is a compendium of many stories
included in his earlier books, each documented with historical background
and information to help in the debunking (and occasional proving true!) of
the legends.

William G. Doty, *Myth: A Handbook* (Westport, CT: Greenwood, 2004).

A lot of books out there about myths aren't written by folklorists, and, as you
now know, folklorists take a very specific view of what makes a story a myth.
This book both acknowledges the folklorist's purist view and goes beyond
it, to give a comprehensive understanding of how the word is used in other
fields as well.

THINGS WE DO

When it comes to things we do, we're entering an incredibly broad
area of folklore studies. Customs (like holiday traditions), gestures
(like a thumbs-up or flipping someone off), parties (like costume
parties or tea parties), rituals (like fraternity or sorority initiations, or bar mitzvahs), celebrations (like sixteenth or twenty-first
birthdays), dances (like the two-step, the "Macarena," the electric
slide, the chicken dance), games (like kick the can, tag, capture
the flag, and four-square[12]) . . . these are all things we do, and
since many of them exist in forms that we learn informally, from
our experiences in regular, everyday life, they fall under the pur-
view of folklore. The quality these things all share in common, of
course, is that they all require some kind of action—some type of
body movement or physical participation in the tradition. Thus,
the modes of transmission for this kind of folklore are largely
observational. Unlike a legend, which can be e-mailed as easily as
told in person, it's not so easy to e-mail someone a Thanksgiving
dinner celebration. Maybe you could e-mail someone an aspect
of the custom, like a photo of the turkey or a copy of the toast
someone gave, but not the whole experience.

This necessary level of engagement makes customs and events
a super-fun form of folklore to study. Try asking different members
of your family to describe a typical holiday celebration—you'll be
surprised how much meaning different people can place on different aspects of a holiday. In fact, it's in traditional celebrations
of holidays that we can see one of folklore's biggest impacts on

the lived experience: anyone who has married or moved in with someone who decorates a Christmas tree differently (blinking lights?! Who would do such a thing?) or who bakes the "wrong" kind of pie at Thanksgiving (pumpkin is, I'm sure we all agree, the only acceptable kind) or who never made green pancakes/beer/ milk on St. Patrick's Day (blasphemy!) has likely experienced the surprising impact that deeply ingrained customs can have on a relationship.

It can be hard to determine clear-cut boundaries for many examples of customary folklore. When does a meal begin—with the cooking or the eating?[13] Does party prep or cleanup count as a traditional part of a traditional celebration? What aspects of the custom are dictated by tradition (foods? words? actions?), and which are nontraditional or up to individual choice (dress? contributions? arrival time?)? These questions can make the documentation and analysis of customary folklore quite tricky.

Imagine that a classmate is describing to you a weekly tradition he participates in, where a number of people gather each week to sing folk songs together. You may assume that you're about to hear a lot of folk songs that your classmate sings, but when you initially ask him to tell you about it, he begins by explaining the group's history, which predates his participation in it. Then, his descriptions of the actual events don't really seem to focus only on the singing—there are desserts made and shared, beverages contributed, inside jokes told and retold, and the crisscrossing relationships of the people in the group—many of whom know each other from different, overlapping associations—often determine the shifting topics of discussion. When you ask directly about the songs they sing, there seem to be some unspoken rules at work: your classmate perceives that some songs "belong" to certain people, while others are more general. He describes a few times when someone clearly "stole" someone else's song and there was notable tension in the group, but when pressed, he claims that no one *really* owns any of the songs, but that they're just sometimes so tied to a particular singer that it might as well be a different song altogether when sung by someone else. He suggests that you join him one week, and you find yourself wondering how successfully you'd navigate the unspoken undercurrents of appropriate interaction.

How would you go about collecting and documenting that weekly custom from your classmate? If you were transcribing his words, at what point in his explanation would you choose to start the "text" section of your documentation? When he described the group's history? When he detailed his initial participation? How would you account for the numerous other folkloric elements of the event—the foodways, the jokes, the folk songs—that emerge from within the overall custom? What contexts would you need to describe—the general context of the weekly gathering, or the individual contexts of each singer's age, gender, skill, repertoire, prior relationships, and longevity in the group? If the same song sung by two different people is so different as to be perceived as a separate song, would you document it twice? Just from this one example, it should be clear that the realm of "things we do" is quite (excitingly) complicated.

When we talk about customary celebrations, we can divide them into two main types: calendar customs and rites of passage. These two forms of custom are distinguished mainly by the way they relate to time.[14]

Calendar customs are cyclical, they happen over and over again, following a regular pattern within the year or the seasons. That can mean a custom happens every year (Hanukkah, Valentine's Day, Flag Day), every quarter (solstice and equinox), every month (date night, book club), or even every week (Pancake Sundays, your classmate's weekly folk song gathering). Rites of passage, in contrast, happen linearly, over the course of a lifetime (like baby showers, getting a driver's license, buying a drink at twenty-one, marriage, divorce, remarriage, retirement, and death). We can envision the temporal difference like this, with the calendar customs on the left and rites of passage on the right:

Fig. 3.1

Along with the difference in temporal movement, there's an equitable difference in function. Calendar customs serve to remind us of the consistencies in life, while rites of passage highlight the transitions. Both of these types of custom can be purely cultural (meaning that the subject of celebration is a human invention: the Fourth of July or being able to drive at sixteen), or they can follow a physical or biological reality (meaning that the event would happen even if people didn't celebrate it: solstices and equinoxes, or the onset of puberty). They can often appear in institutional forms that are celebrated in folk ways (a family's Fourth of July BBQ tradition while observing the city's fireworks display overhead), or in entirely folk forms (small-scale things like Pancake Sunday or first-day-of-school celebrations, things that may not be celebrated outside of that group at all).

Rites of passage are especially interesting because throughout time, a consistent pattern has emerged in the way that groups of people acknowledge these transitions in life. Whether they're a biological reality or we've just made them up, the turning points in human beings' lives often bring about a sudden change in social status or a shift in responsibilities. As many teenagers have thoughtfully observed, there's really very little difference between someone at fifteen years 364 days and someone at sixteen. And yet, legally and socially, that single day makes a world of difference. There's a whole new realm of life to engage in, and a whole new set of responsibilities that come along with it. This is where rites of passage come into play—the celebration can help transition birthday boys or girls by providing them with a physical enactment of their otherwise conceptual or abstract status change.[15]

Rites of passage typically fall into three stages. The first is where the subject of the celebration is separated out from the rest of the crowd and identified as unique. We can see this stage in everything from a birthday boy or girl being made to wear a funny hat to an initiate into a secret society being asked to wear ceremonial dress or abstain from normal activities. The second stage is defined by its in betweenness (folklorists like to use the word *liminality*, as "liminal" means "in between," and as it sounds more academic than *in betweenness*, which isn't actually a word anyway). This is where we see crazy fun stuff happening—all conventions go out the window. We spank people for their birthdays, eat and drink in copious quantities, act silly and out of character—all the stuff we typically associate with "celebration." Because this middle stage is so often equated with normalcy being turned upside down, folklorists will often use the word *carnivalesque* to describe the types of things that go on.[16] The final stage is when the subject is reincorporated back into regular everyday life, but with a greater ability to accept the new role or new responsibilities that come with the new stage of life. The rite of passage helps the transition feel less arbitrary.

It's important to note that the middle stage, the liminal stage, is really the most interesting. This is where folklorists get to jump in and apply all sorts of cool theoretical ideas about the ways that humans function in groups. One particularly cool idea is that in the liminal middle stage of a rite of passage, not only are norms and conventions set aside, but all cultural identifiers are dropped—things like class and gender and relationship status. So, during these times we may see children ordering their parents around, we may see dressing down, dressing up, or cross-dressing, we may even go around kissing strangers. Folklorists have theorized that this loss of identity is what allows a new identity to be donned when the celebration is over—we have to be undressed before we can put on new clothes. Some folklorists also think that the occasional release afforded by rites of passage helps maintain order the rest of the time. Knowing you can cut loose and go crazy once in a while makes it easier to maintain order on the whole.

We can see this three-part structure on both large and small scales, even for the same transition point. Take engagement, for example. On its own, the entire period of engagement could be seen as the middle stage of the rite of passage of marriage—the point where the couple is in between singledom and marriage. Or, we could look at a specific celebration during this time, such as a bachelor or bachelorette party, and consider the three phases of that event: when the person is singled out as the focus of the party (the bride- or groom-to-be may be made to wear silly clothing or identifying accessories), followed by the carnivalesque celebration itself (which may include excessive consumption of food and drink, flirtatious or licentious behavior, or the purposeful embarrassment of the bride or groom), and then the reincorporation into normal life, better prepared socially for the upcoming change.

An interesting thing to consider is the way in which this often-unconscious pattern, once recognized, is used by groups that want to consciously create a new identity for someone. Whether it's a fraternity or sorority bringing in new pledges, an office bringing a new employee into the fold, or even a family welcoming a new in-law, there are often rites of passage that consciously follow this pattern, incorporating symbols that reflect the group identity into the custom.

When I was a student, I attended Memorial University of Newfoundland (a good school for folklore studies). Newfoundland is an island off the eastern coast of Canada, and Newfoundlanders—a culture with a wonderfully strong and self-aware sense of group identity—have developed a rite of passage[17] that they employ to turn visitors and outsiders to their culture into "honorary" Newfoundlanders. The process, referred to as getting "screeched in," involves a number of activities that use many stereotypical markers of Newfoundland identity: kissing a dead cod fish, eating local food like cods' tongues, wearing a fisherman's coat or hat, standing in a bucket of seawater,[18] drinking a locally made rum,[19] and reciting a complicated sentence in an extreme local vernacular speech and accent. The symbolism of Newfoundland identity that's employed in the screech-in is completely over the top, and isn't necessarily representative of all (or even many!) Newfoundlanders (just as the stereotypical American love of apple pie and baseball doesn't neces-sarily apply to most individual Americans). The screech-in has been criticized by many Newfoundlanders as offensive and demeaning, and yet the tradition persists.

This is an excellent example of a rite of passage that is not what it seems to be on the surface. It consciously uses all the tropes of a rite of passage to transition a person from one state to another (from a non-Newfoundlander to a Newfoundlander), though all parties involved are fully aware that the honoree has not in any way become a *true* Newfoundlander, even at the end of the ceremony. And while the symbolism appears to play to a potentially offensive stereotypical image of a Newfoundlander (a cod fisherman who eats questionable food and speaks unintelligibly), the undercurrents of offense are more complicated them simple mockery. A fellow student of mine explained her opinion that the screech-in isn't offensive by observing, "First, Newfoundlanders, in general, can take a joke. Secondly, we can laugh at ourselves along with others. Third, we know that the way in which the Newfoundland 'screecher' is portrayed is not at all representative of Newfoundlanders or of the province as a whole. The joke thus falls on the outsider."[20] So, despite appearances, we have neither of the two most obvious possibilities for analyzing or understanding this custom. It's not a genuine initiation, nor is it an offensive mockery of the local culture. It's a complicated mix of purposes and meanings, and the goals and outcomes are likely different for insiders and for outsiders. As simple as the idea of a rite of passage may be, there's typically more going on than meets the eye.

Here's a fun thing to try: take a moment and consider what a rite of passage to make someone an honorary person-who's-from-where-you're-from would entail. What foods would you make someone eat, what clothing would they wear, what would they have to say or do to embody a generalized local identity? How much do you yourself conform to the stereotypical identity that you'd construct for your hometown or school or region or state? How much more accurate would the representation be if you were creating a ceremony to induct someone into your family versus your city or state? Considering these questions highlights the level of complexity that goes into any analysis of customary folklore.

Want to Know More?

Arnold Van Gennep, *The Rites of Passage* (London: Routledge and Kegan Paul, 1960).

This book, first written in French in 1909, is the one to read if you're interested in rites of passage; almost all other studies written since reference it. If you find the three-part breakdown interesting, this is where you'll find a full elaboration of the concept.

Jack Santino, *Halloween and Other Festivals of Death and Life* (Knoxville: University of Tennessee Press, 1994).

If calendar customs interest you, then this is a good resource to check out.

The focus of the collected essays is (obviously) on Halloween, but hey, it's one of the most fun holidays, and there is good generalizable information on the concept of seasonal festivals as well.

THINGS WE MAKE

When most people think of folk objects (often referred to as "material culture" by folklorists), they usually think of handmade goods: furniture, tools, clothing, quilts, decorative cross-stitching, and the like. Handcrafts are, indeed, one of the most studied forms of material culture. For a long period of history, if you wanted something you had to make it; one result of this is that the qualities of folklore (variation and tradition) were easily found in many of the objects that people had in their homes—they had learned the general form and style of furniture from those around them (tradition), and through varied levels of ability and creativity they'd add their own individual touches (variation).

These days, we get most of the "necessary" goods in our lives from commercial rather than social processes, and so any obvious folk qualities in things like furniture, tools, and clothing are diminished. As much as you want to claim that your IKEA chair is based on a traditional Swedish form, it was still produced (if not put together) in a factory somewhere, identical to all other chairs produced the same way.

The stuff that the majority of us tend to make by hand these days is usually (though not always) the unnecessary stuff—paper airplanes, crafts, yard art, and so on—and it's in these types of creations that we can still find a lot of folk variation. Interestingly, the materials used for these kinds of objects are often appropriated or found objects: jewelry or accessories made from food wrappers, yard sculptures made from bottles or old machine parts, notebook paper transformed into airplanes or cootie-catchers.[21] Rather than the romantic idea of harvesting and hand-hewing the goods we need from the natural landscape, our contemporary material culture reflects our contemporary reality: we're finding creative ways to use junk and excess and make it an expressive component of our lives. This is absolutely a form of "traditional material culture," just as much as a handmade object made from natural substances.

Not only do mass-produced objects become folk objects when they are turned into something else, but even when they are used in an unexpected, traditional way we can start to identify them as a part of folklore. Ever gone on a trip and taken a small toy or figurine with you to photograph in different places? Ever seen all the pictures online of garden gnomes on vacations in different spots? This tradition of travel mascots[22] is another way in which a mass-produced object can become a folk object, and some institutions have even picked up on the process. The Flat Stanley project,[23] in which schoolchildren draw a picture of a flat boy and then mail him to faraway family and friends with a request for photos of Stanley in different spots, is basically the commodification[24] of the folk travel mascot model.

Collections of objects, or, to use a fancier term, assemblages,[25] are another example of this phenomenon. Since people rarely go around designing and making their stuff by hand anymore, we see people expressing their material individuality through the traditional practice of collecting things: souvenirs, spoons, magnets, shot glasses, and even more unusual things like colorful socks or midcentury lamps. Anything that involves the bringing together of a set of like objects can qualify as a traditional collection, whether the likeness is found in theme, function, source, or whatever. We also see group collections, compiled not by an individual but by a bunch of people together, like the collection of candles, figurines, notes, and flowers that appears at spontaneous shrines to memorialize accident victims.

In addition, mass-produced items can become traditional in the way they are passed on: items of family history that are handed down generationally, prank pass-around gifts that regularly go back and forth among families or between two friends, bookcrossing books[26] that are passed from reader to reader. This emphasizes one of the more important aspects of resituating a mass-produced object as a folk object: there needs to be some kind of repeated pattern. Keep in mind that an object can be important and meaningful without being a "folk" object—we're going to need some evidence of both tradition and variation in order to call it a folk object, and looking for a repeated pattern can help us do that.

The pattern that helps us identify a meaningful object as specifically a *folk* object can be a pattern of use (an object is repeatedly used at certain times and in certain ways, like a travel mascot or a special platter brought out for every holiday dinner), a pattern of creation (a type of object that is created regularly, over and over again, like a paper airplane or bubblegum-wrapper chain or a collection that's always growing), or a pattern of passing on (an object that has been continually handed on, shared, or circulated among a group of people, like a family heirloom or a pass-around gift). Once there's a pattern there, we start entering into the realm of tradition and open the door for the possibility of variation.

Imagine that you're planning to collect material culture from your own family members, and after you explain the concept to them, they deliver to you a variety of objects: a friendship bracelet made by your sister, a necklace that once belonged to your great-great-grandmother that your mother wears every year at the holidays, and a small dog figurine that your nephew bought with his allowance and gave to your brother for his birthday. Clearly you've got a variety of meaningful objects in front of you, but determining whether or not they're folk objects isn't the easiest thing. All three of these things are clearly very personally meaningful within your family, and if you interviewed the donors you'd get some really great explanations of how the objects came into their lives and what makes them meaningful. In order to determine if you're dealing with folklore, though, you'll want to consider each object with regard to the patterns of use, creation, or passing on that they all entail.

The friendship bracelet is pretty straightforward, right? There's obviously a pattern of creation: this object is handmade, using a technique that your sister learned from her friends on the swim team, and this individual bracelet, like all the others she's made, uses a common and easy-to-produce design that your sister has enhanced with her own creative embellishments and color choices. Other girls on the swim team make similar, but not identical, bracelets on a regular basis. There's tradition in the style and technique, and variation in the color choices and unique pattern of knots. Clearly a folk object.

What about the necklace? It once belonged to your great-great-grandmother and now it belongs to her great granddaughter, your mother. It's not handmade—it probably came from a jewelry store, though no one knows for sure. There's the possibility that you can find a pattern of passing on here, since the necklace once belonged to an older family member and now belongs to a younger, but your mother admits that her great-grandmother didn't necessarily set the necklace aside for her, and neither did any of the generations in between. It was simply kept in the family, and when your mother discovered it in her mother's things, she kept it for remembrance. That leaves us with a possible pattern of *use*—is this object used in a way that makes it traditional? It seems it is: your mother wears it at the same time every year, at the holidays. She doesn't wear it all the time, or even often, but she subscribes to a repeated, traditional use of this object as part of her celebration of a calendar custom. The necklace, through its pattern of use, has become a folk object.[27]

Which leaves the dog figurine. Initially, this one may seem similar to the necklace—it's not handmade, so there's no pattern of creation, and while it was given as a gift, there's no pattern of passing on regularly. Is there a pattern of use? Let's imagine that your brother tells you that ever since he got the dog figurine from his son, he's kept it on his bedside table. This isn't really a pattern of use, it's more an issue of consistent display—the object may be meaningful, but there's no pattern that involves any action or intent on your brother's part, not in the creation, use, or passing on of this object. Survey says: not a folk object.

Now, this is a very fine distinction, right? It wouldn't take much to add in an element that would instantly transform this meaningful, nonfolk object into a meaningful folk object. Perhaps your brother decides he likes the gift so much that he's going to start a collection of dog figurines. Every time he finds one, he'll add it to the collection, and the family will quickly learn of his interest and start buying them as gifts for him, thus starting a pattern of creation. Or perhaps your brother begins a tradition of taking the dog with him whenever he travels for work, and reporting back to his son all the adventures the dog has while away, thus creating a pattern of use. Or perhaps your brother will wrap the small dog up in a giant, misleading box for Christmas and return it to his son, or pass it on to another family member, with the expectation that it will continue circulating through the family, thus creating a pattern of passing on. In these ways, the dog figurine could easily become a folk object.

As should be clear now, folk objects are different from the word- and action-based genres in several ways—the variation and repetition that we look for as markers of "folk" status don't manifest in the same way, since objects have physical permanence in ways words and actions don't. This lingering quality, while it may make it harder to witness dynamic variation, does offer a significant benefit. When someone finishes telling a story, it's gone; when someone finishes using a piece of jewelry, compiling a collection of objects, or making a candy-wrapper chain, it remains. It may be dropped, perhaps considered lost, but it's not gone. Material culture can exist separately from the people who create it, and that makes it an excellent record of the past.

Want to Know More?

Henry Glassie, *Material Culture* (Bloomington: Indiana University Press, 1999).
   This is a wonderful comprehensive approach to the study of material culture. Glassie covers the methods of material culture study and then provides examples of his own work to illustrate his ideas (and includes pictures!).
James Deetz, *In Small Things Forgotten: An Archaeology of Early American Life* (New York: Anchor Books, 1977).
   This book is written by a historical archaeologist who aims to illustrate how paying attention to everyday material culture can illuminate an understanding of the past. Especially useful to students of history, Deetz's book covers everything from pottery remnants to vernacular architecture. You'll never look at all the stuff in your house the same way again.

Michael Owen Jones, *The Handmade Object and Its Maker* (Berkeley and Los
    Angeles: University of California Press, 1975).
This book presents an interesting portrait of a single folk artist, a maker of
Appalachian chairs, and his creations. It shows the depth of understanding
that can be gained from a single, focused case study, and stands in contrast to
the more comparative method that folklorists often employ.

THINGS WE BELIEVE

As I explained earlier, the category of things we believe overlaps
with all the other forms of folklore quite regularly. As a discrete
form of folklore, however, the phrase "folk belief" is commonly
understood to refer to superstitions, legends,[28] and beliefs about
the supernatural. Now, there's one very important thing to note
at the outset of any discussion about folk belief, and that is that
folklore can be true. It certainly isn't always true, despite often being
believed, but the classification of something as folklore does not
mean that it's specifically not true.

   This is one of those preconceived notions that folklorists are
constantly working against—"folklore" is a word that in common
use is dismissive: "Oh, that's just folklore!" Think back to what we
said about legends just a few pages ago; they're told as true, right?
Well, some of them are true, and some of them aren't.[29] Whether
they're true or not isn't the reason folklorists are interested in them;
all folklorists care about is that they are shared among a group
via word-of-mouth transmission, prompting us to ask why they
remain popular. Rarely does the answer have to do with the literal
truth or untruth of the story. So while it's a popular pastime to test
or try out various folk beliefs and legends,[30] the final determination
is mostly just an interesting side note next to the social and cultural
forces within a group that keep a story, custom, or belief afloat.

   For a long time in the history of folklore scholarship, supernatural folk beliefs were one of the forms of folklore that allowed
scholars to see themselves as superior to "the folk"—clearly anyone who believed in such ridiculous things as good-luck charms,
curses, fairies, ghosts, Bigfoot, vampires, werewolves, and the like
were simply uneducated and deluded by the traditional beliefs of
their equally misguided communities, right? Wrong, as it turns out.

Just as we now understand that everyone is folk, we also understand that everyone—even scientists!—has folk beliefs. Whether they're to do with luck, the supernatural, the nature of the universe, religion, or whatever, all people have folk components to their beliefs systems, components that work in tandem with their more official beliefs to create a functioning and complex system.

People often assume that as scientific understanding increases, folk belief in the supernatural will decrease. This seems to make sense—as we come to understand the scientific mechanisms behind natural phenomena, we'll no longer need supernatural explanations—but this isn't borne out in fact. Supernatural belief hasn't declined much at all in the past century despite incredible advances in science, and as with all folklore, it's the job of folklorists to show up and start asking why.

The field of folklore studies offers two alternative explanations for supernatural belief: the *cultural source hypothesis* and the *experiential source hypothesis*.[31] According to the first, a person who subscribes to a particular supernatural belief does so because his or her culture has said that it's true. In other words, if you grew up in a family or community or culture that tells you that Bigfoot roams around in the forest on the edge of town, then you'll believe in Bigfoot. Perhaps in the woods one day you might imagine that you see a mysterious figure or hear a strange noise, and you'll assume it's Bigfoot, whom you've been culturally prepped to believe in.

The other option is that instead of culture being the source for a belief, actual experience is. Let's consider Bigfoot again.[32] If you have grown up never having believed in Bigfoot (or Sasquatch, or the Yeti, or the Skunk Ape), you may still find yourself, out in the woods one day, encountering or observing something that you can't explain. You go through the possibilities: could I be hearing and seeing a regular kind of animal? Could I be disoriented somehow? Could I be mistaken? If you can't find another explanation, you may conclude that you may have seen Bigfoot or, if you've never heard of Bigfoot, you may decide that you've seen some other creature that you have heard of, or perhaps an unnamed monster (and in that case, it might actually be more reassuring to be able to put a name like Bigfoot to it!).

The difference between these two hypotheses is clear: according to the first, the source of supernatural belief is cultural; according to the second, the source of supernatural belief is an actual experience. Often, there's a bit of both in any given belief scenario—culture supplies the name "Bigfoot" and the expectation of that creature's habitat and activities, while a genuine unexplainable sight, sound, or sensation leads to the application of that cultural info to a specific experience—but there are some important implications of both approaches that we need to be aware of.

For a long time, the cultural source hypothesis was all that folklorists had to work with; it was assumed that people believed in supernatural things because their culture told them to believe in them. While there is undeniably an element of culture in many supernatural beliefs, this unfortunately carries the implication that the people in question aren't very smart—that they're deluded or led astray by their traditional beliefs. Thus, the experiential source hypothesis has had a huge impact on folklore studies, for two main reasons. One, it shows that people who believe in supernatural things aren't just dumb or deluded or crazy. Sometimes they are *rationally perceiving a real situation*, even if their interpretation of that perception can't be verified.

In addition to giving people some credit for being thoughtful and rational, the experiential source hypothesis also shows that sometimes folk beliefs are actually onto something—when a belief exists cross-culturally, and the sources of the beliefs are largely experiential, there may be a real thing happening. This has been borne out in a number of studies, most notably folklorist David Hufford's work with the Old Hag tradition.[33]

There is a traditional belief in Newfoundland[34] (and in other places, but Newfoundland is where Hufford started studying it) of a frightening creature called the Old Hag who comes into people's rooms at night, slowly approaches the bed, and then sits either on the bed or on the person, crushing or suffocating them. Hufford interviewed lots of people who believe in this creature, and they reported that when they see the Old Hag they are definitely awake and not dreaming, and that they can't move, they're totally paralyzed. Only when they're finally able to make even the slightest movement—twitching a finger, maybe—do they break free.

Now here's the thing: Hufford started giving lectures on this Newfoundland folk belief at different universities and colleges, and it wasn't long before students began coming up to him and saying thing like, "I've never heard of this Old Hag you're talking about, but I've totally had that happen to me!" This is where we start to see that the cultural source hypothesis isn't enough to explain this belief—how could someone who'd never heard of the Old Hag experience it? Hufford began interviewing tons more people, those who'd heard of the Old Hag and those who hadn't, and found that an enormous number of people had had this terrifying experience. The ones who were familiar with the tradition could easily classify their experience, but those who had no cultural explanation simply filled in the blanks with their own interpretation of what had happened: demon attack, haunting, evil spirits, very realistic nightmare, and so on.

What Hufford found in the end is that people experiencing the Old Hag are experiencing a sleep disorder called "sleep paralysis with hypnagogic hallucinations." And not only were his informants genuinely experiencing something, they were also describing it almost as accurately as modern medicine has been able to do, though some people were using cultural language rather than medical language.[35] What can we take from this? That sometimes folk beliefs represent a rational, intelligent assessment of reality. While culture plays a role in belief, so does real experience. This is a far cry from the days of assuming that people believe in stuff because they are uneducated or simple.

The giant squid—once a legendary creature from sailors' tales and now a marine museum curiosity—is another great example of the role that rational experience plays in the formation and propagation of supernatural beliefs. By listening to the stories of giant squid sightings, and by paying attention to the consistencies in timing, weather, and oceanic conditions, marine biologist Fredrick Aldrich was able to obtain fifteen specimens of a creature that many people thought didn't actually exist.[36] Clearly there is value in considering the possible experiential sources of folk beliefs.

Now, does this mean that every single folk belief is just waiting to be proven scientifically true at some later date? Probably not. But what it does mean is that we can't dismiss these things, and we can't assume that people who subscribe to supernatural beliefs are somehow less intelligent or less rational than others.

If you're out in the world collecting folklore and you run into people who begin telling you stories of ghosts they've seen, aliens they've encountered, demonic possessions they've witnessed, or creatures they believe are living on the edges of their community, the single worst thing you can do is scoff at them. For one, it's insulting, and folklorists should never be rude. But more than that, you stand to miss out on something really interesting. It's very easy when you encounter supernatural folk beliefs to dismiss them, especially if you yourself aren't inclined to believe in such things. But it's imperative that you remember that people can be *rational* without being *correct*. You don't need to agree with their conclusions about what they witnessed or experienced in order to accept that they may be *accurately describing* what they witnessed or experienced. They may use terminology that is specific to their cultural background, but that doesn't mean that their culture is the only possible source for their belief.

Despite what many people think, few people jump to supernatural conclusions—it's much more common that people consider natural or scientific explanations for unexplained events before deciding that it must have been supernatural. Giving your informants the benefit of the doubt that they are being rational, intelligent human beings is one of the best ways to approach the collection of supernatural folk beliefs.

You'll probably also run into people who classify what they feel is "supernatural" in ways you don't—many people who scoff at the notion of aliens and vampires may fully believe in ghosts and angels because in their perceptions those are aspects of religion, not the supernatural. It can take careful investigation to parse through an individual's belief system. It also appears that when it comes to basic things like luck superstitions (you know the ones: black cats, ladders, mirrors, rabbits' feet, etc.), humans may actually be hardwired to buy into them. Behavioral psychologist B.F. Skinner (famed creator of the "Skinner Box," aka the operant conditioning chamber) found that even the humble pigeon gives into the urge to re-create ritually a situation in which a random lucky occurrence happens.[37] When researchers would randomly drop food on the pigeons, they'd observe the pigeons later attempting to re-create whatever it was they were doing when the food appeared, apparently in the hopes of making it appear again. Apply this to sports fans, and you've got the brain mechanism behind never washing your lucky socks, since your team won its first game when (and maybe because!) you were wearing them. I am not in any way intending to pejoratively connect sports fans to pigeons in psychological functioning—the fact is that we *all* give in to the desire to control the uncontrollable through traditional means. Even while our rational brains are scolding us for being ridiculous, many of us still find ourselves backing out from under ladders, knocking on wood, forwarding that chain letter, and tossing salt over our shoulders, just in case.

Want to Know More?

David J. Hufford, *The Terror That Comes in the Night: An Experience-Centered Study of Supernatural Assault Traditions* (Philadelphia: University of Pennsylvania Press, 1989).

This is an incredible illustration of the importance of paying serious attention to folk beliefs. Hufford's work combines careful fieldwork with insightful interpretation, and is one of those books that makes you look at the supernatural in a different light. It also has lots of fun, scary stories about the Old Hag in it, so it's an enjoyable read.

Wayland Hand, ed., *Popular Beliefs and Superstitions from North Carolina*, vols. 6 and 7 of *The Frank C. Brown Collection of North Carolina Folklore* (Durham, NC: Duke University Press, 1964).

You may be able to find this collection only in the reference section of your library, but it's worth the search. It's a classic example of old-style folklore collecting: superstition after superstition, listed and numbered and (occasionally) attributed to a person or region. You'll be amazed at what you'll learn.

Diane Goldstein, Sylvia Grider, and Jeanie Banks Thomas, *Haunting Experiences: Ghosts in Contemporary Folklore* (Logan: Utah State University Press, 2007).

With a focus on contemporary ghost beliefs, this readable collection of essays highlights the fact that supernatural belief is here to stay. Topics range from science to gender to haunted real estate (did you know that some states require you to alert buyers to the fact that your house may be haunted?).

NOTES

1. William A. "Bert" Wilson first suggested this division. You can read more about it in his collected essays (*The Marrow of Human Experience*, ed. Jill Terry Rudy [Logan: Utah State University Press, 2006]).

2. Remember the two-part job of a folklorist: to collect folklore and then to analyze it. This chapter offers some concise examples of this process.

3. Folklorists prefer the term *narratives*, as it sounds more academic.

4. So much so that these are often referred to as the "major" genres of folklore, while the shorter forms are the "minor" genres; this is not because the major one are more important, but simply because they've been studied more.

5. An urban legend, or, as folklorists prefer, a contemporary legend, specifically.

6. Folklorists have shortened "friend-of-a-friend" to FOAF. It's a fun word.

7. This version of AT 545B is highly abridged. And FYI, "AT" is short for "Aarne-Thompson," an awe-inspiring classification system for folktales. Look for a book called *The Types of the Folktale*, and prepare to be impressed. And to start referring to stories by number. Antti Aarne and Stith Thompson, *The Types of the Folktale: A Classification and Bibliography*, FF Communications 75, no. 184 (Helsinki: Academia Scientarium Fennica, 1961).

8. It's very important to note that "told as true" is not the same as "believed to be true." The legend derives its impact from being presented as literal truth, but that same presentation also invites doubt, questioning, and criticism. This is exactly what we're supposed to do with legends; it's folktales that we're not meant to be skeptical of.

9. At least when it comes to folk transmission. We don't tell folktales orally to each other much anymore, but they're incredibly popular subjects for books, film, and television these days.

10. Aside from jokes, which we unfortunately don't have space to address here.

11. Or any kind of folklore, really.

12. The kind of four-square you played as a kid with a ball, not the kind you play on your phone.

13. Or perhaps even with the shopping for ingredients?

14. That's pretty neat, right? Makes folklorists seem like physicists!

15. If, at this point, you're cleverly noticing that "birthdays" as a customary celebration are sort of both a calendar custom and a rite of passage—good for you! Birthdays are unique in that they happen yearly and yet are also a transitional point in one's life. When it comes to the study of folklore, however, it's really only the culturally significant birthdays (sixteen, eighteen, twenty-one, fifty, sixty-five, etc.) that get treated as full rites of passage, because the shift in social expectations is so much greater for those years. And, of course, that list really only applies to contemporary American culture—in cultures and times where other birthdays coincide with culturally or legally significant changes, those would be the big years.

16. Think of Carnival, or, as it's better known around here, Mardi Gras, and you'll get the idea.

17. This kind of consciously created tradition is known as an "invented tradition." Invented traditions can easily become "real" or "authentic" traditions over time, but the term implies an awareness that originally, this was constructed with the intent of becoming folklore, which often makes folklorists wary of assuming that the functions and implications of the event are genuinely representative of the folk group.

18. Are you catching the emphasis on fishing yet?

19. The rum is called Screech, after the noise an early taster made when sampling it, and provides the ceremony with its name.

20. Alicia Cox, "Screech In or Screech Out?" *Transmission* (Memorial University of Newfoundland) 7, no. 2 (2005): 6.

21. Remember cootie-catchers? Those little fortune-telling things you'd make with paper? They had four chambers to put your fingers in, and you could open and close them in different directions and unfold different tabs to reveal different messages. Those were fun.

22. Do a Google image search for "travel mascots" or "roaming gnomes" if you don't know what I'm talking about here. An interesting aspect of this tradition is how it's now being reappropriated back into mass culture: movies, television shows, and commercials have all featured the roaming gnome tradition. The travel company Travelocity's spokes-gnome is now so ubiquitous that many people think the connection between gnomes and travel started there, rather than the business having appropriated a folk tradition.

23. Check out www.flatstanley.com.

24. When folklore is appropriated by the mass media or manufacturers, folklorists refer to that process as the "commodification of folklore," since a folk item is being turned into a commodity that can be bought or sold. We can also see the opposite process taking place, such as when we make a mass-produced toy into a travel mascot (or take movie lines and make them into inside jokes with our friends). I like to call this process the "de-commodification of pop culture." Share and share alike, right?

25. This term has slightly different meanings in different contexts. There is the general understanding of the word in English to mean an assembled group of things, and there is also the way the term is used in art (where it is typically pronounced in the French way), which indicates a creative process that utilizes found materials to create a work of art. Both uses of the word can apply to the folk process of compiling objects into an expressive collection.

26. Check out bookcrossing.com.

27. It can be tricky to reconcile the idea of an individual's customary wearing of a piece of jewelry with the understanding that folklore is, by definition, *shared* among a group, but take a step back and consider the bigger picture. It's unlikely that your mother has never heard of anyone else in the world having a special item that is worn or used only on special occasions—this is a common type of behavior in our society. It's similar to the way that an individual sports fan's wearing of a lucky shirt—itself unique to the individual who owns it—can still be classified as a folk belief or superstition. The shared cultural expectation that individuals have

lucky items or special jewelry that are brought out at traditional times is what makes this process folk.

28. This one is genuinely double-booked as something we say and something we believe, as evidenced by its definition as a narrative that's told as true—the possibility of *belief* is at the heart of a legend.

29. A great example of a true urban legend is a story that circulated widely via e-mail and by word of mouth a few years ago about a pregnant woman who was stopped in a sporting goods store and accused of stealing a basketball. The managers made her stop and show them her pregnant stomach before they were willing to accept that she wasn't smuggling a basketball under her shirt. So she sued them. True story!

30. Mythbusters, Snopes.com, and a ton of people on YouTube are all evidence of this.

31. These opposing hypotheses have been described at length by a famous folklorist named David Hufford. Check out the "Want to Know More?" list at the end of this section for a recommendation of some stuff of his to read.

32. No, I do not know if Bigfoot really exists—sorry. That's beyond the scope of my expertise as a folklorist.

33. David J. Hufford, *The Terror That Comes in the Night: An Experience-Centered Study of Supernatural Assault Traditions* (Philadelphia: University of Pennsylvania Press, 1989).

34. You've probably noticed that lots of folklore work comes out of Newfoundland—you should visit sometime!

35. Lots of people say that Hufford has "explained away" the supernatural belief with medical jargon, but that's really not the case. What he's done is show the connections between the traditional and the institutional languages used to describe the same phenomenon, and noted that both are equally accurate. We should wonder why we assume that the medical phenomenon "explains" the traditional belief. What if the traditional belief explains the medical phenomenon? Rather than saying that someone experiences the Old Hag because they have sleep paralysis with hypnagogic hallucinations, maybe people experience sleep paralysis with hypnagogic hallucinations because the Old Hag has come to visit. Think about *that* when you're falling asleep tonight.

36. He did this partly by posting "Wanted!" posters all over the place, which nearly got him in trouble with his university. Can you imagine a zoologist or a biologist today putting up posters saying, "Wanted, Dead or Alive: One Unicorn!"? They'd be fired.

37. Skinner, "'Superstition' in the Pigeon," *Journal of Experimental Psychology* 38 (1947).

Chapter 4

Types of Folk Groups

It may seem a bit arbitrary to pluck just a few random folk groups from the vast array of possibilities to talk about here, but too bad, because that's what we're going to do. There are some groups that folklorists have studied more than others, and it's more likely that a student in a folklore class will have the opportunity to collect from some groups rather than others, and the examples here reflect those realities. In this chapter we're going to look at folk groups based on work, age, beliefs, and interests, considering some of the main types of folklore that crop up in them. If you're interested in a folk group that's not discussed here, that's okay—it's likely that you'll still gain some insights that can translate.

Remember that a folk group is half the equation of folklore: when folklorists looks at a given folk group, they're seeking the folklore that exists within that group as a means to better understand that group as a cultural unit. While certain types or genres of folklore may exist more in one kind of folk group than another (college students may be heavy on the legends while a workplace may have many customs), it's important to note that any kind of folklore can appear in a given folk group: to say that there's such a thing as "occupational folklore" or "campus folklore" is not to say that these are types of folklore distinct from other genres such as legends, jokes, and customs. It's simply to apply a shared theme (occupation, education) to all the legends, material objects, and customs that can be found in that group. It's important to keep the distinction between "folk" (the group of people) and

DOI: 10.7330/9780874219067.c004

"lore" (the genres or forms of expression) straight: a folklorist can approach the field from either or both of these angles, starting with a particular group (college students), a particular type of folklore (political jokes), or the intersection of both (political jokes told by college students).

We should also remember that many folk groups have both folk and institutional components to them. Occupations have the rules and regulations of the company, along with the stuff that a new employee learns informally from coworkers on the job. Religions have the doctrinal expectations for believers, along with the cultural expectations that come from the community rather than from the officials. In these instances, the word *alongside* is often used to describe the relationship between the folk and official cultures of the group. Folk religion exists alongside the institutional aspects of a religion; occupational folklore exists alongside the business's rules and regulations. This emphasizes an important fact about the culture of folk groups: the folk culture is no more or less important than the official culture.[1] It doesn't exist above or beneath the official culture, but right next to it, affecting how we act toward, interact with, and react to the other people in the group.

My students one semester came up with a great example of this: the cultural knowledge we have about driving a car. The folk group here is a broad one—people who are licensed drivers. On the institutional level, members of this folk group are aware of the many legal requirements for drivers: that they be licensed and that they take an official test in order to become so, that they obey traffic lights and speed limits, that they wear a seatbelt and have working turn signals and lights, and so on. On the folk level, we have the common folk belief that you are allowed to drive up to five miles per hour over the speed limit without getting a ticket,[2] we have the custom of kissing your hand and hitting the roof of your car when you drive through a yellow light, of lifting your feet when you go over train tracks or a cattle guard, of holding your breath through a tunnel or past a cemetery. We know that cars with only one working headlight are called padiddles (or perdiddles, spadoodles, or padinkles), that the proper acknowledgment for being allowed to merge ahead of someone in heavy traffic is a friendly wave, and that we pass time on long car rides by playing the license plate game (or the punch buggy game). All this folk knowledge exists right alongside, and is employed at the same time as, the official knowledge.

Of course, not all folk groups have an institutional level to their culture: families, for instance, rarely have a truly institutional level to their culture—everything is on the folk level. The same goes for groups united by more abstract concepts: knitters, high-school cliques, fishermen, mothers, really tall people . . . remember that a folk group is made up of any two or more people who share at least one thing in common. Lots of groups created by that definition aren't going to share an official culture.[3] That's okay—a group, especially a smaller group,[4] can get by with only folk culture quite easily.

OCCUPATIONAL FOLK GROUPS

Occupational folk groups were one of the earliest areas of folkloristic inquiry in this country. Since America didn't have a peasant class in quite the same way as European countries did, American folklorists turned to various occupations, especially labor-intensive occupations like lumberjacks, steelworkers, or firefighters, in search of traditional expressive culture. Of course, they found a treasure trove of lore: work techniques that are learned on the job rather than through formal training, lingo and jargon pertaining to tools and skills, legends of especially great (or especially awful) past workers, customs for initiation into the labor force or ascension to a new rank, and so on. Occupations create intense shared identities—especially when the work is risky or dangerous and workers have to rely heavily on each other for safety—and any time there's a shared identity, there's usually folklore to reflect and reinforce it.

Even in jobs that aren't labor intensive, however, there's still occupational folklore. Many office or service industry workers learn within their first few weeks how things actually work—whom to approach for help or with questions, whom to avoid about certain projects, when to follow procedure and when not to, how long a break actually lasts, which customers are notorious and how best to treat them—and this sometimes ends up being the more important skill set, at least on a daily level.

A student of mine once collected a story from her coworker about a past employee who had been simply *terrible* at his job. He was so terrible that he didn't last long, and by the time she collected the story he hadn't worked at the organization for many years. His popularity as a subject for conversation and storytelling, however, was undimmed by the passage of time. Certain mistakes that he was infamous for had been named after him and specific instances of his ineptitude were so familiar to current employees that his name became synonymous with them. Employees would say things like "He's a new Dave!" or "Watch out for Dave v2.0!" when someone would make a mistake, or they would warn each other, "Don't pull a Dave!" when it seemed that someone might be headed toward a misstep. Stories like this[5] are clear cautionary tales; when a new employee hears the story, or even when longtime employees rehash it over and over, it's a symbolic reminder to not act like Dave, to not do what Dave did or make the kind of mistakes Dave made. Personifying incapability helps illustrate incapability, and provides a group of employees with a neutral (well, neutral once Dave didn't work there anymore, at least) character through which to offer advice, give warnings, and reflect norms and expectations. Workplace stories like this serve as ongoing training and education, reaffirming the values of the business and the expected traits of its employees.

Rites of passage are also a popular form of folklore in the workplace, as people are often arriving as new employees or being promoted to new levels. My students have told me stories about new movie theater projectionists being made to drink shots of popcorn butter, apprenticed butchers being dunked in cow's blood, and new customer service reps being prank-called by coworkers with purposefully unanswerable questions—these initiations help bond new employees to old ones and can create a sense of camaraderie. One great example of a workplace rite of passage was at Henry Ford's "English School" graduation celebration during the early 1900s. Since Ford hired so many immigrant workers, he wanted to find a way to unite them all and ease their transition into American culture. His school taught not only the English language but also American customs and manners. For the graduation ceremony, the workers would exit a large model of a boat (representing their arrival as immigrants to the United States), and then enter into a giant "melting pot" wearing the traditional dress of their home countries. They would eventually emerge from the pot wearing a business suit and waving an American flag.[6] It seems strange in this day and age, when we are taught to respect and encourage diversity, that so obvious an effort would be made to culturally homogenize a group of people, but it's an excellent example of the power of a rite of passage in the workplace. Ford found a need to unite his work-force, and he consciously created a folk custom in order to do so.

Similarly self-conscious forms of occupational folklore—wherein a company decides to institute a tradition for its workers to share—exist today. Casual Fridays, monthly office lunches, and promo-tion and retirement parties are common examples of office customs that, while they may be initially fabricated, can grow into genuine components of an office's culture. Seeking the ways in which folk-lore grows organically in a workplace and comparing that to the purposefully invented traditions can help to highlight the nature of an occupational experience in a unique way. Business students would do well to consider the utility of occupational folklore stud-ies to their future endeavors.

Imagine that you're interviewing a coworker about your shared occupational folklore. You bring up the monthly office tradition of going out for drinks on the final Friday of each month, a cus-tom that you felt helped you to get to know your colleagues when you first joined the company, and that you feel reflects a friendly, cohesive office community. Your coworker, who has been working at the company longer than you have, has a different perspective. She tells you that not long before you arrived, your boss decided that she wanted to encourage her employees to be friendly with each other and basically forced everyone to postpone their weekend free time once a month and put on a show of being friends rather than colleagues for an hour or two. No one had wanted to do it, your coworker tells you, and everyone basically resents the fact that while they're not "officially" required to show up, they pretty much have to if they want to stay in the boss's good graces.

How does this affect your perception of the custom, which you genuinely appreciated and considered successful at creating group cohesion? Is your coworker simply cynical, or are you blind to the actual attitudes of your officemates? Is your boss a responsive leader with a belief in office friendships, or a manipulative aggressor imposing her will on her underlings?

People spend enormous amounts of their lives at work, and the culture (and folk culture) of the workplace is therefore an important element of modern life. Some folklorists have begun using the concept of "organizational folklore"[7] (another way of saying occupational folklore, but with an emphasis on complex corporate structure) as a form of public-sector work, taking academic theories and putting them to use on behalf of human resources departments trying to best serve their employees.

Want to Know More?

Robert McCarl, *The District of Columbia Fire Fighters' Project: A Case Study in Occupational Folklife* (Washington, DC: Smithsonian Institution Press, 1985).

Robert McCarl is one of the leading experts on occupational folklore, and this book, published by the Smithsonian, is a classic example of the study of workers' folk culture. It's amazing to learn how much there is to know about being a firefighter that has little to do with fighting fires—the true breadth of occupational folklore is featured here.

Archie Green, *Only a Miner* (Champaign: University of Illinois Press, 1972).

Archie Green, another leading scholar in the study of occupational folklore, presents the culture of coal miners through a consideration of their traditional working songs. Some are well-known tunes, some are esoteric and unfamiliar, but all of them reveal how the life of a miner can be captured uniquely in the expressive form of song.

Michael Owen Jones, "Why Folklore and Organization(s)?" *Western Folklore* 50 (January 1991): 29–40.

This article is one of the first to take on the question of occupational folklore in the office-based workplace, related to but distinct from the folk culture found in situations of manual labor. This study pushed the boundaries of this folk group to a new place. Business students should check this one out.

RELIGIOUS FOLK GROUPS

When it comes to religious belief, folklore gets really interesting (and tricky), for a variety of reasons. One, if you go around calling someone's religious beliefs "folklore," you're asking for trouble, given the general misconception that folklore means "not true."

Two, it can be problematic to talk objectively about religious issues with anyone—folklorist or otherwise—who has his or her own personal faith. Between these two potential pitfalls, however, there's a lot of fascinating stuff to be learned here.

What is religious folklore? Rather obviously, religious folklore is the stuff that emerges from a religious group but that isn't determined by the institutional levels of the religion. A typical example of this is saints' legends in Roman Catholicism. While much of saint lore is codified by the Catholic Church, there's a lot that isn't. Take, for example, the burying of a saint's statue in your yard in order to force the answering of a prayer (St. Anthony for finding romance, St. Joseph for selling your home, etc.). The Catholic Church has never officially put this plan forward as a recommended course of action, but if you ask people why they did it, or why they believed it would work, they'd answer that it's because they're Catholic. It's an element of noninstitutional (aka folk) religious belief.

Catholics aren't the only ones who have noninstitutional aspects to their religious practice and belief. Muslims in need of luck or protection may seek out a *marabout* (a holy person, though the term can also refer to the tomb of a holy person) to procure an amulet or blessing, even though this practice is considered unorthodox. Contemporary Jewish people may similarly carry a talisman to protect against the evil eye. Practitioners of syncretic Vodun (Voodoo) traditions may create mojo bags to heal specific maladies or repel curses. Religious objects like these can run the gamut in meaning and use from kitschy tourist gift to sincere object of belief, and can even fill a role somewhere between the two.

We can see this multilayered meaning playing out at Shinto shrines in Japan. Shinto is the indigenous religion of Japan, and many of its practices constitute a folk religion, as there is no official governing institution for the belief system. Many Shinto shrines and temples will offer patrons paper fortunes called *omikuji*, which contain predictions of luck ranging from terrible to wonderful. It's a common folk practice to tie one's fortune to a tree or fence outside of the shrine, either to leave bad luck behind or to increase good luck. Tourists and locals get in on the tradition in equal measure, and the trees near some Shinto shrines end up nearly enveloped by

Fig. 4.1

the small pieces of paper. Knowing that this custom is performed by a range of people from a range of belief systems for a range of reasons, it is hard to generalize about the function and meaning of this particular custom. Individual believers have very personal relationships with both the institutional and folk aspects of their religions, and careful fieldwork is necessary to fully understand any instance of faith.

There are also examples of folklore that aren't actually about a religious topic but that emerge from within a religious folk group, and so become associated with that particular religion. Members of many faiths, for example, often associate certain foods with certain religious holidays, leading to an identification of the food with the religious celebration, even though there is no institutional requirement that that specific food be consumed during the event.[8] Among Utah Mormons, there's a popular side dish called "funeral potatoes"[9] that takes this connection ever further. The potatoes themselves have no religious meaning (and they are served at non-funeral events, too), but they've become a clear cultural marker of that particular religious group. If you were to ask people why they make funeral potatoes, or how that tradition became a part of their lives, they'd say that it's because they're Mormon, or because their families are Mormon.[10]

There are some terminological distinctions that can help clarify the difference between these two types of religion-based folklore. The term *religious folklore* applies generally to all the folklore, belief-oriented or otherwise, that is shared by a group united by religion (like funeral potatoes). The term *folk religion*, in contrast, is more often used to describe beliefs and practices that are religious in nature but not defined by the official dogma of the church or belief system (like saint burying). Sometimes you'll find the two terms being used interchangeably,[11] but it's good to have the distinction in your mind.[12]

We also need to remember that people who do not identify with any institutional religious group may still have folk religion, even though there's no official canon for their beliefs to exist alongside. People may have a belief in a deity or deities, in the existence of spirits or angels, or in the power of prayer, all without subscribing to any particular religious doctrine, and they may even have legends and memorates[13] that support their beliefs, and customs that they share with other noninstitutionally spiritual people. Even the phrase "spiritual but not religious," which is a new shared identifier for many people, is itself a form of folklore.

Considering that many people both leave and join religions in their lifetime, and that religious groups often overlap with regional groups, there's also the possibility that people may be able to report on the folk religion or religious folklore of a group that they're no longer a part of, or on a group that they're culturally affiliated with but not religiously affiliated with. A student of mine once attempted a collection project with a local branch of the group known as the Post-Mormons,[14] people who have left the Mormon religion and are seeking advice and companionship during their transition out of the religion. My student was very interested in what kinds of stories and beliefs this group would share—she quite reasonably expected that there would be a traditional batch of "Why I left" stories, stories that might share themes of doubt, disillusionment, or growing unease with the teachings of the church.

Interestingly, she found no such stories. What she *did* collect were a bunch of faith-promoting Mormon stories, legends that the group members recalled hearing back when they were active members of the Mormon Church. They were all stories that my student could have collected if the folk group she'd worked with had been current satisfied members of this religion, and yet they all came from a group specifically defined by its break from that religion. Clearly, while the Post-Mormon group members had left the Mormon *religion*, they were still quite embedded in the Mormon *culture*. And of course, while the legends themselves were the same, the intent behind the telling of them—the significance of the stories to the group and their function within it—were drastically different. Rather than being faith-promoting legends, they were viewed in this new context as falsehoods, perceived as stories designed to blind followers to reasonable doubts and contradictions. This is an excellent example of the importance of context and texture to the meaning of a narrative; looking at the text alone could be extremely misleading when trying to discern what a legend might mean to its tellers.

Want to Know More?

Don Yoder, "Toward a Definition of Folk Religion," *Western Folklore* 33 (January 1974): 2–15.
> As indicated by the title, this article deals with the basic definition of "folk religion." Yoder describes a range of historical attempts to define this field of study and brings aspects of them together in his own succinct definition.

Leonard Norman Primiano, "Vernacular Religion and the Search for Method in Religious Folklife," *Western Folklore* 54 (January 1995): 37–56.
> This article presents an important alternative view for the study of religious folklore. Primiano disagrees with the dichotomy of "institutional" and "folk" religion, believing that it overlooks too much and does a disservice to individual believers, within whom the reality of religious experience resides.

Dennis Covington, *Salvation on Sand Mountain: Snake Handling and Redemption in Southern Appalachia* (Philadelphia: Da Capo, 1995).
> Written by a journalist who begins his investigation in a courtroom and ends up joining a snake-handling church, this book explores the nature of unconventional religious belief and conviction. It's a great example of how mainstream and folk religious practices blend in an individual's experience.

CAMPUS FOLK GROUPS

College campuses offer a wealth of folklore, and if we consider that one of the things folklore can do for a group is to offer social and psychological support and release during times of stress, then we see immediately why this is true. Consider some of the most enduring college legends: if your roommate dies, you get an automatic A in all your classes, right? What about that music major who died right before graduation—supposedly you can still hear her ghost playing the piano in the concert hall at night. Did you see that one test by the guy who gave an incredibly clever and creative answer to a question about thermodynamics by talking about how a girl told him she'd date him "when hell freezes over"? and got full credit, even though the answer was wrong? Or have you heard that if your professor doesn't arrive within the first fifteen minutes of class, you're legally allowed to leave and can't be docked points?[15] And wasn't the library built upside down, or backward, or by two warring architect brothers who each designed half the building with no regard for matching what the other was doing? Say, did you hear about that one kid who totally openly cheated, and then stuck his bluebook in the middle of the stack and got an A because his professor didn't know his name? Yeah, I've heard them all, too, as have thousands of college students across the country.

These legends sum up the myriad stresses that the average college student has to deal with on a regular basis. Social and emotional stresses seem nigh unbearable in the face of academic stress; it's a relief to think that the extreme of the former (your roommate dying) would be softened with a removal of the latter (guaranteed straight As). Professors hold an enormous power over their students, and it's satisfying to think that there's a limitation on that power, or that students can outwit their professors and get the upper hand once in a while. Even without a story of warring architects, college campuses are often a hodge-podge of building styles and pathways—it's nice to think it's not that you can't find your way, it's that the campus is poorly designed.

Take this legend, for example: two college seniors decide to take a break from studying for finals and spend the weekend partying hard. Unfortunately, they party so hard that they over-sleep Monday morning and miss their chemistry final. They agree on a story and approach their professor with their explanation: they had taken a trip over the weekend and got a flat tire on their way back. As they didn't have a spare tire they had to wait for res-cue and thus missed their final exam. Their professor takes pity on them and offers to write them a new final exam (since they could easily find out from classmates what had been on the original) and let then take it later that day. The two guys are thrilled with their success, but when they show up to take the final they're pre-sented with only one question, worth 100 percent of their grade: "Which tire was flat?"

This legend, told often about a specific professor at Duke University and purported to be at least partially true,[16] has circulated since at least the late 1970s and has been set at a number of dif-ferent colleges. So what's so appealing about it? Well, it's a nice tale of comeuppance, for one. These two cocky guys think they're smarter than their professor, only to find out that he's managed to outsmart them. While we might have expected their trickery to work in their favor, we instead get a reassuring message that the way *we've* been doing it—studying long and hard and showing up on time—is in fact the best path to success.

What about this one? Bored students in a psychology class decide to turn their professor's own lectures against him by con-ducting an experiment in positive reinforcement and behavioral conditioning. They slowly begin to shape the professor's actions by acting very attentive only when he does certain things, like stand on the left side of the room or puts a foot up on the trash can. Whenever he does anything else, they talk, fidget, and act uninterested. By the end of the semester, they've got the professor lecturing from on top of the trash can!

We get a totally different message here than we do from the story of the flat tire. In this scenario, the students win—not only do they manage to play a prank on their professor, but they're actually illustrating how adept they are at employing the very concepts he's supposedly an expert on. This is clearly an appealing idea to students—who wouldn't want to believe this was possible?

The scales are so regularly weighed in the faculty's favor[17] on a college campus—power over grades, over passing or failing, over recommendations, over internships, over enrollment—that it's a relief to hear about a situation in which that power structure is overturned. In contrast to a system-supporting message in the first legend, we get a rebuttal to the norm in this one. Both together start to paint a picture of the nuanced issues being addressed and reflected by campus legends.

Whether it's providing wish fulfillment or the articulation of an underlying anxiety, campus folklore clearly both reflects and helps to negotiate the college experience. Rites of passage are another of the most common ways this happens. Not only within fraternities and sororities—where initiation rites are at times infamous—but in many general campus populations there are traditions that allow for the fast and furious bonding that intense social and academic pressures require. When you meet your new dorm mates, you know that these people are going to be present for your most crazed cramming sessions, your most embarrassing emotional collapses, and your best parties. The sooner you can bond with them, the better. Many campuses have developed quasi-institutional customs that meet these needs, such as campus-wide celebrations during the first week of school, Homecoming activities, pregame rallies, and dorm-specific theme parties. At other times, the students themselves develop customs in which the school officials play no part.[18]

Knowing the insider culture of a campus is in some ways similar to occupational folklore, in that students quickly learn the unofficial ways to navigate the institution. Sharing insider tips on getting into the most popular classes, learning how best to BS on a test you didn't study for, knowing which areas of the library are the best for napping, where to go for the best parties, how to get the most food for your money from the cafeteria . . . when people look back on their college days, it's often this stuff that they remember as much as (if not more than) the content of their classes. The folk culture of campus life is an enormous part of the overall college experience.

Want to Know More?

Simon Bronner, *Piled Higher and Deeper: The Folklore of Campus Life* (Little
    Rock, AR: August House, 1995).
    Bronner brings together previous research and his own fieldwork for this
    compilation of campus-specific folklore. He applies a range of approaches to
    understand the material, and it makes for a fun overview of student life.
Elizabeth Tucker, *Campus Legends A Handbook* (Westport, CT: Greenwood,
    2005).
    This book goes beyond just legends (though it has a good number of those,
    too) to talk about all kinds of campus folklore. Tucker's straightforward pre-
    sentation offers ideas for analyzing and interpreting the folklore in the unique
    context of the academic setting, too, and her book serves as a great accessible
    example of folkloric analysis in general.

CHILDREN'S FOLK GROUPS

Children's folklore is awesome for one main reason: the population
of this folk group is constantly changing, and yet the folklore it
generates is some of the most consistent and long-lived folklore out
there. It's bizarre—considering that the people who qualify as "children"[19] are changing every single year, you'd think that the folklore
they share would be equally changeable. Nope. Not at all. Consider
the fact that kids have been playing Ring around the Rosie[20] and
London Bridge[21] for decades, if not centuries, and you get a sense
of the longevity.

Another interesting thing about children's folklore is that it's
one of the rare folk groups in which all adults have at one time
been a member. An unfortunate result of this is that it's very easy
for adults to feel that they completely understand children's culture, perhaps better than the children themselves do. This is an attitude that most people would never presume toward any other folk
group; how patronizing it would be to look at members of another
culture and claim to understand them better than they understand
themselves![22] With children, however, that condescension seems
more acceptable—they're young, not yet fully developed mentally
or physically, and so it's not a true judgment of capability to say that
adults know better. The problem is that while adults certainly were
at one point members of the culture of childhood, they no longer
are, and it can't truly be said that the adult imagination is capable

of genuinely recalling the experience of being a child, at least not in the way that a child perceives it. Folklorists need to be constantly reminding themselves that children are a unique, fully formed culture all on their own, and not simply unfinished adults.

We can see examples of this rich folk culture when we look at the way that children can be extremely crafty and clever in their play. I'm sure everyone remembers one or two of the rhymes that kids use to choose an "it" for a game, right? Eeny-meeny-miney-mo, catch a tiger by the toe, and all that jazz? Well, then perhaps you'll also remember the common situation in which you were rhyming your way through your playmates and it became obvious to you that you were about to end the rhyme on an undesirable "it." What to do? Add a verse to the rhyme, of course! "My mother says to pick the very best one and you are going to be it!" Or, if that one leads you to the wrong "it," too, you can say, ". . . and you are *not* going to be it," thus starting the rhyme over again. It's great to see how a tradition that's ostensibly for the purpose of introducing randomness into the selection process can be turned against that goal.

Children also have a ruthless sort of ranking system that emerges in their traditional games. Remember playing house? The selection process for who gets to be parents and who has to be kids (or pets!) is always interesting, as is the way in which roles are easily dismissed after being fought for. We can see in children's traditional games a reflection of their perception of adult life—the roles, the rules, and the social expectations into which they're going to have to assimilate at some point. The really cool thing is how those expectations are just as often obliterated by children's folklore as they are upheld. We grown-ups could probably learn something from that.

Children are always doing things in ways that mystify adults—the world assumes one course of action and children regularly take another. This is exemplified in children's material culture—the ways that children play with their toys. Folklorist Jeannie Thomas has studied the things that children do with their Barbie dolls—not only the expected (and commercially supported) activities of dressing them up and playing with their official accessories (houses, cars, companions, etc.), but the real things that real children actually do, like rename them, undress them, remove their heads (the toilet seems to be a typical repository for dolls and doll heads), hack off their hair, cross-dress them, combine them with toys from unrelated toy lines, and so on. One of Thomas's informants has a specific type of favorite Barbie play that involves Barbie getting into accidents over and over again—she is blown up, run over, or drowned.[23] These are presumably not the typical situations that the designers of Barbie had in mind when they envisioned their impossibly feminine dolls being used by children, but it's what many children actually do with them. There is a whole world of creative play with mass-produced toys that children engage in and learn from each other that has nothing to do with mass-produced goals or intentions—children's folklore culture is a far weirder place than many popular representations acknowledge. This distinction between what the media portrays as children's culture and what children's culture is actually like makes for interesting analysis.[24]

Want to Know More?

Brian Sutton-Smith, Jay Mechling, Thomas W. Johnson, and Felicia R. McMahon, *Children's Folklore* (Logan: Utah State University Press, 1999).

This interdisciplinary collection of essays and resources is a must for anyone interested in pursuing study of children's culture. It provides a history of the study of children's folklore, many examples of different genres of folklore, and a discussion of methods and approaches.

Iona Opie and Peter Opie, *The Lore and Language of Schoolchildren* (New York: New York Review of Books Classics, 2000).

This is an older book (originally published in 1959), but it is still an amazing compilation of children's folklore. You'll find almost four hundred pages of riddles, pranks, rhymes, beliefs, rituals, superstitions, games, customs, taunts, nicknames, and more. Given the age of the book, the familiarity of many of the types of folklore included will help highlight the impressive consistency within this ever-evolving folk group.

DIGITAL FOLK GROUPS

Wait, what? "Digital" folklore? I know, I know—it seems strange to connect something like tradition to something like technology, but don't let your preconceived notions about folklore outweigh what you now know to be true: folklore is informal traditional culture and has nothing to do with being old or quaint or rustic. These days, we do much of our informal daily socializing on our computers or phones and, quite unsurprisingly, folklore has shown up there, too.

In 2002, a guy named Mark Prensky coined the term *digital native* to describe everyone[25] born after the year 1980.[26] What he meant by this is that people born after that date have never lived in a world without digital technology—computers, cell phones, video games, and the like. The most interesting implication of this (for a folklorist, at least) is the basic suggestion that there is a digital *culture* out there that one can be native or nonnative to.[27] Just as with any other linking factor, online interaction can be at the root of a folk group, and this particular type of folk group is a kind that more and more of us each year are increasingly affiliated with.

We should take the time to note that there are several different types of digital social interaction. There are offline folk groups that have an online presence—a family might share a blog or several blogs, a campus club might have a Facebook page, and a local group of young mothers might have a Web forum where they share Web links and post pictures. Of course, nonlocal moms might find that Web forum and want to join in, too. Or maybe there wasn't ever a local, physical group that met in person—maybe the group was started online by a mom who felt isolated and wanted to seek out advice and camaraderie. This bridges us into another kind of digital folk group: the kind that exists only online. One isn't better than the other, but a complete understanding of any group is going to require that you understand the extent of the group's connections. If you lurk around a popular Web forum that is its members' only way of connecting, then sure, you might be getting a picture of their entire cultural interaction.[28] But if you're lurking around a site that's the digital component of an otherwise analog (offline) folk group, then you're only getting a partial picture. Lots of students assume that digital fieldwork is going to be easier than traditional fieldwork because it can be done from home while in your PJs, but that's not always the case.

When we look at what kind of folklore appears in digital settings, we often find that it's just old folklore in a new guise, such as the urban legends or jokes that circulate via e-mail or as text messages. We tend not to see genres such as folktale or myth crop up in virtual settings (at least not in folk circulation—there are a lot of online repositories, however), but we do see things like folk speech (slang, abbreviations) and customs.

Digital culture has given us a whole new language to decipher—lol, rofl, ily, bff, imho, tptb, ftw, fwiw, icymi, etc.—and a whole new set of text-based "gestures" used to indicate tone and attitude.[29] For digital natives, there's a significant difference in the meanings of these three sentences:

> Hope your day goes well :)
> Hope your day goes well :/
> Hope your day goes well ;)

In the first, a genuine well-wishing is taking place. In the second, there's clearly some knowledge that the speaker has about the recipient's upcoming day that compromises the possibility of the day going well—the speaker is offering support and acknowledging that there is a reason the day may be difficult. In the last example, there is again an unspoken understanding on the part of the speaker; this time the tone is playful or teasing, as if the speaker knows of a reason that the day might go especially well indeed. As with all folklore, there's no guidebook for how to use these emoticons—it's something you learn from observation and experience. You only have to send a winky-face to the wrong person once before you learn never to do it again.

When it comes to customary traditions online, we have things like the understanding that certain information belongs in a private message on Facebook rather than on someone's timeline. One of the markers of someone being new to a social network like Facebook is that he or she puts the wrong types of communications in the wrong places (like a generic "Hey, friend, long time no see, here's what's been going on, hope you're doing well" greeting in the comment section for a specific photo or status update). Just as in the offline world, where people learn from experience and observation what kinds of things to bring up in public and what kinds of things to say in private, or what kind of things to bring up as a point of order at a meeting versus over drinks after work, our online social spaces require the same kind of folk cultural knowledge.[30]

Of course, not all forms of folklore on the Internet are forms that also exist IRL.[31] Some forms of digital folklore are new genres altogether, ones that make use of the mixed media available through technology. Internet memes—images, phrases, or concepts that spread rapidly over the Internet[32]—are one great example. We have pictures, videos, and text, all being used together to create personal expressions that then are appropriated and adapted by others and put back out there for further re-creation. The qualities of variation and tradition are extremely easy to see in this form of digital folklore—some elements are notably conservative and some are notably dynamic. For as "new" as this kind of folklore may seem, it's a great way to practice the basics of folklore identification. Consider the evolution of the "X all the Y" Internet meme, which began with this frame of a Web comic from the blog Hyperbole and a Half.[33]

The original Web comic was a reflection on the initial enthusiastic ambition one often feels to clean one's house (followed by the inevitable dismay at realizing how many things there actually are to clean), and quickly got picked up by others who began altering the message.

Here's one inspired by the Beatles:

And one in honor of a popular NPR show:

One that clearly grew from the ever-popular theme of the zombie apocalypse:

One about the Internet's favorite topic[34]:

And one made for a folklore class by one of my students:

The conservative elements let us know that all these images are part of the "same" tradition, but the dynamic elements express a variety of interests, themes, cultural trends, and affiliations.

Overall, one of the main things we find in digital folk culture is a blurring of the barriers between the levels of culture, so that we get mass-media techniques (film, photography, graphic editing, far-reaching broadcast, etc.) used in the creation and sharing of folklore. We also see a blurring between the genres of folklore, so that we have images and words and actions all coming together in a single form. Is an Internet meme something we say? Something we make? Something we do? Or all three? It's still very much a folk process, just on a different (and generally intriguing and exciting) scale.

Want to Know More?

Trevor Blank, ed., *Folklore and the Internet: Vernacular Expression in a Digital World* (Logan: Utah State University Press, 2009).

While a few individual articles and book chapters had come earlier, this is the first compilation of academic essays to directly address the topic of folklore on the Internet. Case studies span from familiar forms of folklore online to digital-only forms of cultural expression.

Trevor Blank, ed., *Folk Culture in the Digital Age: The Emergent Dynamics of Human Interaction* (Logan: Utah State University Press, 2012).

This book, a follow-up to the previous volume, offers readers more case studies that show the interesting, important, and useful ideas that studying online folklore can reveal.

Nancy K. Baym, *Personal Connections in the Digital Age* (Malden, MA: Polity, 2010).

Baym's book serves as a straightforward introduction to the idea that meaningful social and cultural interaction can take place through technologically mediated communication. Readers get some clear, theoretical concepts to help them think about the subject, and several historical and contemporary case studies to illustrate the social and cultural validity of online interaction.

NOTES

1. Though the penalties for breaking the rules of official culture may be more specific than for breaking the rules of folk culture.

2. This is, unfortunately, not true.

3. And in truth, many of them may not even share folklore. There are innumerable potential folk groups created by this definition—women who wear a size 7 shoe, for example—that while they may exist nominally, do not actually interact exclusively enough to generate a definable folk culture. Make the link a rarer feature, though—say, women who wear a size 11 shoe—and perhaps that characteristic is rare enough that people who share it have sought each other out (to share tips on where to buy shoes, maybe). Just be aware of both the benefits and the limitations of this broad definition of folk group.

4. This is one reason why folklorists have often chosen to study smaller groups rather than huge ones.

5. They'd be classified as legends if told in the third person, and as "personal-experience narratives" if told in the first person—remember, folklore can be true!

6. Applying the three-part structure of a rite of passage here is interesting: what happens in the pot, during the middle phase? The previous identity is stripped (along with clothing), but the new one hasn't yet been put on. What a strange moment that must have been!

7. Michael Owen Jones, "Why Folklore and Organization(s)?" *Western Folklore* 50, no. 1 (1991).

8. This makes for a fun exercise. Think of the religious holidays that your family or your community celebrates, and consider what foods it simply wouldn't be that holiday without. See if you can discover where the emphasis on that food came from, and whether or not it has any official connection to the theme or purpose of the holiday.

9. In case you were wondering, the genre that folklorists use to describe food-based traditions is "foodways." And also, the potatoes are sometimes called "cheesy potatoes."

10. If you doubt the localized importance of funeral potatoes to Utah Mormons—Google it. It has its own Wikipedia page.

11. Isn't it fun how ambiguous all the terminology used in folklore studies is?

12. Not all folklorists are on board with the term "folk religion." Check out the recommended reading by Leonard Primiano at the end of this section for a more nuanced discussion.

13. A "memorate" is a first-person belief narrative. Basically, it's a personal-experience narrative that's told about a supernatural subject. If the same story were told in the third person, it would, of course, be a legend.

14. Visit www.postmormon.org for information, if you'd like.

15. And if the class is taught by a TA or grad student, you have to wait only ten minutes!

16. Check it out on Snopes.com—they asked Prof. Bonk himself.

17. Well, from a student's perspective; ask the faculty and you'll get a different story.

18. It is interesting to consider when school officials choose to ignore unsanctioned campus traditions (like pranks, parties, rumors, unofficial holidays, etc.) and when they finally decide to take action. The fact that things usually have to get pretty bad before anything happens—students injured or property damaged—shows that school officials see the value in preserving folklore within their institutions.

19. This is an incredibly ambiguous and subjective term, by the way. When does childhood start and end? At a particular age? Is it a particular stage in life, regardless of age? If the answer to these questions has changed over time (which it has), then how do we classify past "children's" folklore? When children worked in coal mines, maybe coal mining folklore was actually a type of children's folklore! It's interesting to mull this one over.

20. OMG, did you hear that it's really about the Black Plague?! Sorry—it's not.

21. And this one's about child sacrifice during construction, right?! Sorry—nope.

22. Of course, anthropologists—and yes, even folklorists—did this for quite some time.

23. Jeannie Thomas, *Naked Barbies, Warrior Joes, and Other forms of Visible Gender* (Urbana: University of Illinois Press, 2003), 155.

24. If you're in a folklore class and are thinking of collecting or studying children's folklore, remember that there will likely be some sort of special permission involved. If your project is going to end up in an archive or anything, there surely will be.

25. Well, more like everyone born in the developed West into a family with enough money to own a computer.

26. Prensky, "Digital Natives, Digital Immigrants," *On the Horizon* 9, no. 5 (2001).

27. It is important to note that being "native" to a culture is not the same as blindly accepting all the generalizations that go along with it. As we noted before, not all Americans love apple pie and baseball, even though those are generalizations regularly made about them. Similarly, there are digital natives who love to write with fountain pens rather than type on a keyboard and who prefer to chat in person over coffee rather than online. Similarly, there are immigrants to digital culture who are way more adept at technology than younger, more native people—it's not a simple either-you're-in-or-you're-out situation.

28. Though you'd likely still be missing out on things like private messages, e-mails, and chats—one thing to remember about doing fieldwork online is that you often aren't aware when you're missing something. Unlike being with a group in person, where you can observe when two people pull away and start talking privately, you'll never know when two forum members start to message each other privately. Only solid ethnographic work can help offset this disadvantage.

29. In truth, the "newness" of these forms is only in perception. The use of a colon and closing parenthesis to indicate a happy tone in text was first suggested on September 19, 1978. (Yes, September 19 is also International Talk Like a Pirate Day—two folk holidays in one!)

30. One of the reasons that digital culture often becomes a contentious topic in contemporary discourse is because it's so relatively new that we haven't yet had enough time to develop widely agreed-upon cultural norms for it. What's considered rude when it comes to the use of cell phones in public? When is it tacky to solicit help or funding for a personal project on a social networking site? What's the protocol for dealing politely with accidental or intrusive reply-alls in group e-mails? We haven't had these technologies long enough for everyone to have simply grown up *knowing* what's rude and what's polite, and so we run into lots of trouble as we figure it out. It'll be interesting to watch consensus grow over the years.

31. In real life.

32. Also known as image macros; see http://knowyourmeme.com/ to get an idea of what we're talking about.

33. See hyperboleandahalf.blogspot.com/.

34. Spend just a little time on the Internet and you'll soon discover that much of it is about cats. The Internet loves cats.

Conclusion
What Do I Do Now?

So, what should you do with your new understanding of folklore now that you've (almost) finished this book? Class assignments aside, the knowledge and skills of a folklorist are (perhaps surprisingly) quite useful in the real world, so let's consider some ways in which you might use them.

One thing that most students discover upon learning the ins and outs of folklore is that they start seeing it everywhere. Stuff that simply never caught your eye before will suddenly jump to the front of your attention and you'll be going, "Hey—is that folklore?" This provides a great next step: start putting your new understanding of folklore to use identifying things as (or as not) folklore. You know how to go about it now—just remember the basic rules that folklore follows: it's variable and it's traditional.

And don't forget the second goal of a folklorist: not just finding but interpreting the folklore. While you're out in the world discovering and identifying folklore, make sure you take the time to ponder what makes these kinds of cultural expressions unique and relevant, how they function in their cultural and social contexts, and what they mean to the people sharing them. If your coworker e-mails you an urban legend, take a moment (after the natural reaction of debating with your lunch pals whether or not it's actually true) to consider what underlying social truth might be reflected in the story. When you hear a political joke at a party, pause in your laughter (or maybe keep laughing, just to maintain appearances) and think about what social function the joke teller intended the joke to have, and what the joke's reception by the listeners communicated in return. At the next holiday celebration, when someone claims that the Jell-O salad wasn't made the "right" way, take a

DOI: 10.7330/9780874219067.c005

moment to reflect on what it means to a family to have mutually agreed-upon "correct" versions of their traditional foods.

In short, remember that thinking like a folklorist involves being both genuinely engaged in and consciously aware of your own cultural contexts—at the same time. You laugh at the joke, gasp at the legend, smile at the custom, and then you think about the meaning of those traditional forms within the group that shared them. It's kind of like having X-ray vision[1]—you're seeing, reacting to, and participating in all the same things as the people around you, but you're going a bit deeper, too, recognizing that there's a whole world of shared understandings being symbolically communicated around us at all times. When this double awareness gains you an insight you'd otherwise have missed—when your awareness of the presence and significance of folklore allows you to engage more successfully with and appreciate the world around you—you'll remember the single most important thing this book has told you: folklore rules.

NOTE
1. That's right, being a folklorist is like being a superhero.

About the Author

LYNNE S. MCNEILL, PHD, is an instructor and director of online development for the folklore program at Utah State University and co-founder of and faculty advisor for the USU Folklore Society.

Index